What Amazon readers have to say about
Reality-Driven Investing

By LivinginBeauty--Five Stars out of Five

"No need to lose money; just do your homework and remember... As Larry Kudlow always says, "Earnings are the mother's milk of stock prices." They are indeed! This handy little guide teaches the same style of investing as Warren Buffet and Ben Graham, the father of investing."

By Amazon Customer—Five Stars out of Five

"...The book is easy-to-read. Definitely worth it."

By Dennis—Five Stars out of Five

"Hits the nail on the head! ....This book...vividly and with statistical facts drives the point home. Read it and search for the facts yourself..."

By Richard—Five Stars out of Five

"Insightful look at investing!"

By David—Good Read!!

...This book is a basic work on value investing. His use of examples is quite good. Well worth it...

Reality Driven Investing

Using Statistics to Make a Difference

Donald L. Hinman

Library of Congress Control Number:		2016917952
ISBN:	Hardcover	978-1-5245-5533-7
	Softcover	978-1-5245-5532-0
	eBook	978-1-5245-5531-3

Print information available on the last page.

Rev. date: 11/02/2016

To order additional copies of this book, contact:
Xlibris
1-888-795-4274
www.Xlibris.com
Orders@Xlibris.com
751965

CONTENTS

REALITY-DRIVEN INVESTING WAS first published in 2014. I wrote it primarily for my family, especially, my two grandsons. I wanted them to get off to a good start investing in the stock market. Surprise to me!! My book start selling to others. The feedback was very encouraging. With the unexpected interest I decided to pursue having my book be sold on a broader basis.

Since, I have spent some time re-writing adding a little insight here and there. Particularly, giving more useful examples of using stock selection software. Without this software my success in the stock market would be limited.

I use VectorVest largely because of the unlimited number of options the software offers. One still does have to have a very good basic understanding what drives stock value and the stock market forces to get the full benefit of the software. Whether you are a beginner or a veteran investor I hope this book will add some valuable insight so you can improve your results.

I do want to thank my wife, Helen, for being willing to spend hours reading my manuscript not only to correct errors but adding valuable content. However, if you find typos or incorrect language I am the one you should blame.

Don Hinman

Written especially for Quintin and Colton, my grandsons,

YEARS OF FRUSTRATION

I HAD ENJOYED many years of success in the business world, when I started investing in the stock market, I assumed in no time using my business experience I would be a successful stock market investor. That is not what happened. I never could find what it was that would allow me to make profitable stock market decisions. Months turned into years as success eluded me. My mistakes included:

- Listening to tips and opinions of others and acting without questioning or even knowing if the information was valid.
- Never did pay attention to stock value. Actually, I didn't have any idea how to determine value. Value, in my mind was more about future potential than about the company's actual financial record.
- Never paid attention to financial reports. That is amazing, as I did pay attention to my businesses' financial reports.
- Never tried to prove myself to be wrong. Never tested my ideas of what was important or others' ideas before using them. Didn't have the means or skill to do so even if I wanted to do it. Most of my notions had to do with what I was told when I was growing up and little to do with my actually paying attention to reality.
- Never gave much thought how I reacted to the news. I just reacted. Often I was buying when I should have been selling and selling when I should have been buying.
- Spent considerable time trying to understand my risk tolerance, thinking it may have something to do with my lack of success.
- Never bothered to learn about stock market behavior. I had a lot of opinions, but no knowledge about how the stock market in general behaved or specific behavior of individual stocks.
- Never learned how to control my emotions and I let them take over my decision making both when buying and selling.

- Never wrote out an investment strategy when to buy and when to sell. Never thought about what facts or statistics are important and should guide my decisions.
- Never paid attention to the business cycle.
- Never knew the presidential election cycle's effect on the stock market.
- Never tried using a computer or stock market software.
- Lastly, I could never shake the doubt I didn't have the resources or the knowledge to be successful. I listened to both professionals and non-professionals telling me it was impossible for the average person to be successful in the stock market.

All this added up to not knowing the difference between a good stock and a poor one. I had just enough success to keep me going, but I never really made any money. Confidence would be followed by frustration. I read a study of 450,000 savers by Aon Hewitt and Financial Engines that found most do-it-yourselfers failed to do well because they were either too aggressive or too conservative. In other words, their emotions guided their investment decisions. This pretty much described me. I would decide I needed to be more aggressive. My results would remain subpar. So I would switch to being conservative. I would then miss out on a significant stock market rise. Very frustrating!! No doubt about it, I was more of a gambler than an investor.

Then I read the book *blink* by Malcolm Gladwell. The book never mentions the stock market. It did make the point—one needs to pinpoint the relevant information when making a decision. Not knowing and sticking to what is relevant leaves a person confused and unable to make a good decision. I set out to discover the specific information I should be paying attention to when investing. Once I discovered what was relevant and was not, suddenly I was experiencing a breakout. I started making money on the stock market.

My wife, Helen, gave me the encouragement to write down my thoughts. I am thankful she did. Writing forced me to organize my thoughts, to crystallize in my mind that which keeps me on a successful investing path.

THEY WILL SAY YOU CAN'T DO IT, BUT YOU CAN

THERE IS A lot of information flowing in from all directions. We are bombarded every hour of every day. There is the Wall Street Journal, Investor's Business Daily and CNBC providing news and opinions. In addition there are local newspapers, talk radio, hot tips our friends, neighbors, and co-workers offer telling us what is important to consider and what we should do. Some of the information makes sense, but more often than not the opinions and information are conflicting and confusing. I have heard it said, the easiest way not to be confused by the news is not to pay attention to it. This is a bad idea. Lack of information is a sure fire way to failure. Failure after failure makes it easy to give up. If you want to be successful, you do have to decide if you want to learn, to have an open mind and then make the effort to master investing. I refuse to believe being a "do-it-yourself investor" is difficult and risky. Old habits and assumptions do have to be put aside, then one must be willing to learn.

I have talked to many people about their investing experiences. Like many of them, my wife and I sought out a stockbroker. To us, it appeared brokers were the experts and could teach us to be good investors. Stockbrokers are quick to point out that the novice investor does not have the time or expertise to be successful. The argument made sense; after all stockbrokers do call themselves investment advisors. Soon it became clear they were salesmen working for a commission. Helen and I discovered their idea of what makes a stock a good stock was no better than ours. They spent considerable time lowering our expectations. The recommendations they gave us were either from their company's sales or research departments.

To convince us they should be in charge of our hard-earned money, each of the stockbrokers spent considerable time evaluating our risk tolerance. It was decided we had a low risk tolerance and were recommended stocks they labeled as conservative. Actually, the stocks were simply low-yielding and low-performing. Over the years, my wife and I have come to understand conservative to mean buying stocks with a high value at a low price. This is something totally different from the stocks our brokers recommended. They did not talk to us about what it is that makes up a stock's value, nor did they try to compare a stock's value with its price.

They did point out their clients who did best were the ones who gave them money and did not pay much attention to their portfolios. Helen and I spent a lifetime paying attention to our businesses, trying to build up assets. Asking us to not pay attention to our stock portfolio ran contrary to our instincts. After taking what seemed to be poor advice from various stockbrokers, we decided the best thing we could do was to learn about investing in the stock market on our own. That has taken time. Some of the lessons were very expensive. Being wrong and losing money can be frustrating.

We once belonged to an investment club. Members would join and, in a short time, become discouraged and drop out. Most would say, "The market is impossible to understand, and I don't have the time or money to learn. Investing in the stock market is nothing more than gambling." They quit believing it could be done.

Fear and confusing information can and has baffled almost every investor. Richard H. Thaler, in his book *Advances in Behavioral Finance,* cites a study in which "the subjects are to imagine that they are portfolio managers." They were asked to allocate the assets of an imaginary portfolio. The first group was given monthly information, the second group was given annual information and the third group was given five year information. The results of the study showed that the more current and detailed the information each group receives, the less able the group was willing to take a risk when making decisions about which stock they should include in their portfolio. Short-term market fluctuations cause fear to creep into decision making. The result is losing the ability to focus on the right information to make a decision.

To be able to find what it is that distinguishes a good stock from a poor stock, Helen and I discovered that using the same method that is used to tell an excellent baseball player from a good player, or even a poor one, worked. There are many professional baseball players who look like excellent athletes. They may appear to be strong and fast, but turn out to be not very good baseball players. It is not their physical appearance that counts, it is the player's statistics that does, such as batting averages, home runs or runs batted in. There is complete agreement—Willie Mays, Mickey Mantle, Babe Ruth, Randy Johnson and Ken Griffey, Jr. were excellent players. Baseball teams, such as the Oakland Athletics, have used statistics drilling down to gain an advantage over teams who use scouts exclusively to judge a player's potential. The Athletics say getting on first base is more important than a player's batting average. They theorize whether a player hit the ball or walked doesn't matter; what matters is the player's ability to get on first base.

Investors need to use the same kind of thinking when searching for statistics that will give them an edge. To do this, you have to be willing to put aside assumptions and previously held opinions and ask questions. Think outside of the box. Put your theories and strategies to the test—do they work? You need to ask, "Have I searched for statistics that will prove my thinking right or wrong?" Is it fear, or is it knowledge or logic that guides me? Am I more comfortable with "common knowledge" or searching for reality? Am I thinking like an investor or am I thinking like a conservative or liberal? Do I fall in line with others' thinking because I am afraid of looking foolish if I don't? Am I objective, or am I easily influenced by those I think are smarter or better off than me?

There is an advantage to not take the first step in answering these questions. The World will seem safer and more comprehensible. However, accepting a safe worldview and failing to look at reality causes you to miss out on opportunities. You can be more. You can take control of your life. If Bill Gates had accepted and been satisfied with his station in life, we might still be waiting for the Internet. Thomas Edison had hundreds of failures when he tried to invent the lightbulb. When he finally succeeded, he was considered a genius. The Edison genius was less about brains, more about determination and a belief he could do it.

I am a small town businessman, I did it. You can do it too and be a successful do-it-yourself investor.

GETTING THE RIGHT TOOLS

THERE ARE OVER eight thousand stocks traded on the various exchanges and over the counter. (Over the counter stocks are the stocks that are not traded on the major stock exchanges.) There is no way to review each stock and sort them without the aid of a computer and stock market software. There is also a need to review stock histories and back-test your investment strategies. (Back-testing is defined as "the use of historical records to test the effectiveness of an investing strategy, rather than actually using money to test a strategy over a period of time in the future.) Up front, you need to buy the proper tools to do the job. I went years trying without the assistance of computer technology. It was a mistake. The job of finding the right stocks requires a computer with stock market software. A successful investor needs to know the characteristics of a stock whose price will grow in the future. You will be using statistical evidence to measure the relevant stock characteristics. As I mentioned in the previous chapter, this is very similar to the Moneyball tactics used by the Oakland Athletics to evaluate baseball players. These are some of the software functions I have found to be essential:

- Being able to access both current and historical information about every stock traded.
- Being able to design and do stock searches.
- Being able to back-test the effectiveness of a stock search.
- Being able to construct stock lists to monitor.
- Gaining access to the most current financials—such as the profit and loss statement, the balance sheet, and cash flow statements—of any company you have an interest in reviewing.
- Being able to compare stocks using several methods.
- Being able to design stock charts to show the information you believe to be relevant when making decisions.

- Being able to find the most current news about any company, industry or economy.
- Being able to determine the institutional and insider ownership of every stock.
- Being able to isolate stock characteristics and judge the effectiveness of the characteristic you consider to be important.

I use VectorVest software. It is easy to use and has the ability to sort through information and do back tests at a rapid pace. The longer I use VectorVest the more I find out what it can do. To be an effective tool you do have to use computer software in a way that communicates a broad array of information to you, so you can understand and use probabilities to predict whether a stock price will rise or fall in the future. You may be disappointed if you use VectorVest only as a stock picker. There are definitely better times than other times for buying and selling stocks. VectorVest allows me to access Yahoo Finance without leaving its website. There are no definite rules that will give you certain outcomes, but as you gain knowledge and a better feel of the stock market, you will be more successful. VectorVest allows me to access Yahoo Finance without leaving its website. Yahoo Finance tracks news for particular stocks plus other stock information and summaries of financial statements. I cannot make a strong enough recommendation to get on VectorVest's website and compare it with other vendors before deciding which system you like best.

Search engines, such as Google, give the do-it-yourself investor access to information and news not available to the average Wall Street stock research department just a few years ago. Computer technology makes it possible to use online stockbrokers who charge very low trading fees. Online stockbrokers also have significant technical information and stock searches available on their websites. I use Fidelity Investments. One of the reasons I like Fidelity Investments is they are able to make instant trades; the trading price is very near to the stock prices quoted.

Computers give me the ability to focus in on the information I want and need to make a good decision. Don't make the mistake I made—buy the necessary equipment and software at the beginning of your investing career, not later. One of my goals in writing this book is to give you some ideas as to what to look for when considering stock market software. I do want to warn you, you still have to think. If your expectation is computers will enable you to put your decision making on auto pilot, you will be disappointed.

BUYING STOCKS IS LIKE BUYING A BUSINESS

WARREN BUFFETT'S RECORD is astounding. Timothy P. Vick, author of the book, *How to Pick Stocks,* points out that since 1965, Warren Buffett has averaged 22% returns. In this same time period, the next highest mutual fund returns are Fidelity Magellan Fund at 16.3% and Templeton Growth Fund at 13.4%. Jonathan Rahbar, analyst at Morningstar, says, "Warren Buffet approaches buying stock like buying a business. His decisions are made based upon his understanding of real value, not his response to current market pressures to make a profit." I have brought several businesses, the reason I do it is to make a return on my investment. To be successful, one must be objective—not subjective. The questions that must be asked and answered are:

1. What are business's earnings?
2. Will the earnings continue to grow in the future? Paying for "blue sky" or goodwill can be disastrous for the buyer. Blue sky is about popularity. Popularity is a subjective measure that can come and go. There is no real way to measure the value of blue sky or popularity—either the company makes a profit or it doesn't. Value is tied to earnings. Earnings is an objective measure of value. The more the earnings are, the more the value of the business is. The less the earnings are, the smaller the value of the company. It is as simple as that.
3. Are the financial statements of the business accurate?
4. Is it the best time to buy the business? Is the product or the service of the business going out of or coming into style? Is the industry the business is in becoming more or less competitive? Are costs rising or falling? Are prices of the product or service able to response to rising costs or competition?

5. What is the current cost of money? (The cost of money is defined as "the interest rate of an AAA corporate bond or the U.S. Treasury bond.) If earnings are less than bonds why take the risk? Just buy bonds. The company's earnings should reward one for taking the risk of ownership.

The stock market has over eight thousand stocks. Each stock only represents a tiny portion of ownership of a company. While buying a share is not buying the whole company, the questions to be answered are the same:

1. What is the earnings per share or the earnings yield of each share? Earnings per share is determined by dividing the total earnings by number of outstanding shares. ($100,000 earnings divided by a million shares outstanding equals $0.10 earnings per share.) Earnings yield is calculated by dividing the share price into the earnings per share. (S0.10 earnings per share divided by a share price of $2.00 equals an earnings yield of 5 %.) The earnings yield can be compared to the interest of an AAA or Treasury bond.

2. What is the potential growth of earnings per share? Earnings yield and future growth of earnings per share determines value. Historical results and past predictions of growth give the best clues about the accuracy of management's future growth predictions. It is crucial to have a realistic assessment of future growth to know a stock's value. Without this it is impossible to determine if the stock price is too high or too low.

3. How safe are the financial statements from adverse surprises? Market failures, fraud, misrepresentations and earnings prediction failures can cause a sudden stock price drop that will take years to recover.

4. Is this the best time to buy a certain stock? The best time to buy a stock occurs when the value of the stock is more than its price and when the market is down. The best time to sell is when its price approaches or exceeds its value and when the market is up.

5. Is the earnings yield of a stock more than the interest rate of a U.S. Treasury bond or an AAA corporate bond?

Reporting requirements for publicly held companies make it easier to find the information needed to determine value. If one wants to be a successful investor there is no excuse for not finding this information. The strategy is to find a stock which is priced low compared to its value, and the stock represents a healthy company.

EARNINGS AND VALUE ARE CONNECTED

E ARNINGS ARE THE cornerstone of a successful business. Its connection to value is very easy to understand. Earnings pay salaries, wages, utility bills, supplies, rent, mortgage payments and all the other expenses needed to run a business. It goes without saying, a business without profits is a business that will soon go out of business. On the flip side, businesses with profits will be around for a long time as earnings pay for future growth and expansion. Earnings per share measure the profit per share.

The most common measure of per share earnings is the price/earnings ratio (the stock price divided by the earnings per share) or PE. The PE indicates how much one dollar of a company's earnings costs in the stock market. For example, if there are two stocks: Stock A has an earnings per share of $9 and a share price of $57; its PE is 6.33 ($57 divided by $9) or its costs $6.33 to buy one dollar of Stock A's earnings. Stock B has an earnings per share of $5 and a stock price of $92; its PE is 18.4 ($92 divided by $5), or it costs $18.40 to buy one share of stock B's earnings.

Stockbrokers' conclusions about PEs are sometimes very confusing. Ask stockbrokers which is better: a stock with a PE of 6.33, or one with a PE of 18.4. Many stockbrokers do not question market forces. They assume the market does a good job of pricing stocks. This leads them to believe that if the market sets prices, then stock prices are a pretty good indicator of value. Consequently, they will try to convince their clients the stock with a PE of 18.4 is probably the better value simply because it costs more to buy a dollar of earnings. I have had brokers tell me the stock market considers stock B a Cadillac. Everyone knows a Cadillac is more valuable than a Chevrolet. To come to the conclusion stock B is the better buy because it costs more to buy than stock A, throws objectivity out the window. About the only safe conclusion that can be made is stock B seems to be more popular than stock A. It is a stock's popularity, not value, that probably causes investors to pay more for a dollar stock B's earnings. Why is stock B more popular? The answer to this question invites many different opinions and little agreement. It also illustrates the human tendency to latch onto a few facts or factors and make a quick decision. There is also an underlying assumption the market is always right. This book is about making money when in the short-term the market is wrong.

To know which factors are relevant which are not, it becomes important to know the difference between popularity and value. Popularity is determined by buying and selling activity. Popular stocks have more willing buyers than sellers. In the short run, popularity will cause a stock's price to rise. When popularity is the consideration, current earnings per share become secondary or many times completely ignored. Popularity purports an element of hope the market is right about value. Hope makes it easy to outsmart yourself. Decisions based on hope often crumble into fear when adversity raises its head, resulting in panic, creating an urge to sell at the worst possible moment. Zigging when an investor should be zagging is disastrous and keeps success at bay. Value must be grounded in solid evidence about the ability to make a profit.

To get past the problems the PE seems to cause, I have found that paying attention to earnings yield is helpful. It gets the investor in the frame of mind thinking about what is the return on my investment. Calculating earnings yield uses the same information that is used when calculating the price/earnings ratio. Instead of price being divided by earnings per share, it is flipped; earnings per share is divided by price. Stock A's 6.33 PE translate into an earnings yield of 15.7%. ($9 divided by $57). Stock B's 18.4 PE translates into an earnings yield of 5.4% ($5 divided by $92). Asking the question which stock has the better return, one with an earning yield of 15.7% or one with 5.4%, invites the same answer, 15.7%.

It is an answer that works favorably with our human tendency to make quick decisions. It is a decision grounded into something solid that make the investor to be more immune to the day to day pricing of stocks. Short term market fluctuations can cause bad decisions. Most fluctuations have little to do with the actual value of a stock. A few down days make it hard to stick with holding a stock. The urge to sell becomes overwhelming. I like to use earnings yields because when a stock price drops, earnings yields go up. This reality puts me into the proper frame of mind when I observe the market's up's and down's. I am able to make sounder decisions. Profits are lost when investors fail to sell at the right time. Earnings yields are a very useful tool, when deciding to sell a stock. (I will discuss this in greater detail in a later chapter.)

The basic principle of reality-driven investing is that the market, at any given time in the short term is seldom right. The market either underprices stocks or overprices them. But in the long term, the market will correct the pricing error. The reality is these are errors give the investor a real opportunity to make a profit that is greater than the average profit the market produces. (There is a caveat: stocks with an earnings yield higher than 30% might be an indication of future earnings trouble.) Earnings yields puts the investor in a position to judge value. Smart investors will use the market pricing realities to their advantage.

GROWTH OF EARNINGS PER SHARE IS WHAT SETS STOCKS APART

EARNINGS PER SHARE growth must not be confused with total earnings growth of a company. A stock market investor is not buying the entire company. The investor is only buying shares or a tiny portion of a company, so it is earnings of each share and growth of the earnings per share that count. The earnings per share are calculated by dividing the number of outstanding shares into the total earnings of the company.

Either the total earnings of a company or the number of shares can change. Changing either will change the earnings per share. It is possible for the earnings of the company to grow and earnings per share to decline. An example is when companies pay their company with stock rather than money, causing the earnings per share to decline. The earnings of a company can remain flat or decline, and its earnings per share increases. This happens when cash rich companies buy back their shares and reduce the number of outstanding shares.

Common sense and a little arithmetic demonstrate how the earnings per share growth affects stock value. Two stocks, Alpha Manufacturing Corporation and Beta Sales Corporation, have a per share price of $25, earnings per share of $2.20 and a PE of 11.4 ($2.20 divided by $25). It will be the growth of earnings per share that will set the value of each stock apart, making one a good buy and the other a poor buy. Assume, for the sake of this example, both companies can maintain the PE of 11.4 a year from now. Alpha Manufacturing's earnings per share are growing at a yearly rate of 3% while Beta Sales earnings per share are growing at a rate of 25% a year.

In the coming year, Alpha Manufacturing's earnings per share will grow 3% from $2.20 to $2.27. Its stock price will grow from $25 to $25.88 ($2.27 times a PE of 11.4). Beta Sales earnings per share will grow 25% from $2.20 to $2.75. Its stock price will grow from $25 to $31.35 ($2.75 times the PE of 11.4). The chances are, because Beta's superior growth, its stock will become more popular than Alpha Manufacturing. The popularity of Beta will lead additional buying activity, causing its PE to rise making the price spread between the two even greater than $25.88 to $31.35.

Institutional investors use a ratio that combines the concepts of PE and growth which is called PEG. PEG is determined by dividing the PE by the percentage growth number of earnings per share. PEG gives an indication if a stock is overpriced or underpriced. The current PEG of Alpha Manufacturing is 11.4 divided by 3 or 3.8. The current PEG of Beta Sales is 11.4 divided by 25 or 0.46. The smaller the PEG number, the more attractive the stock is. A rule of thumb is, a PEG above 2.0 is overpriced. A 2.0+ PEG will cause reduced buying demand and increased selling pressure, driving the price of the stock down. Likewise, a PEG under 2.0 will increase the buying demand, increasing pressure to drive the price up. This is another value indication making it wise to choose Beta's stock over Alpha's.

How accurate are the earnings per share and projected growth of earning per share? It is a question that must be answered.

SAFETY: THE MISSING LINK

NONE OF WHAT has been discussed is important if the future estimates of earning and growth are not reliable. To be successful there needs to be an answer to the question: How safe are the company's current earnings per share and growth of earnings per share from deterioration in the future? The integrity of financial reporting is essential. Many have lost their life savings because they depended on Enron's or WorldCom's financial statements to be an accurate reflection of the company's financial condition.

There are many ways to cover up financial problems. A company can fail to write off uncollectible accounts, which will overstate their sales. It can fail to take unsellable inventory off their books, understating their expenses. Management can inflate sales by aggressively reporting sales before they are actually consummated, improving their earnings. Banks may be slow to report loan payment problems. Insurance companies may understate reserves on claims that will be paid in the future. Certain industry groups, such as restaurants and clothing manufacturers and retailers, are prone to be affected by consumer fads; so a good year is no guarantee that the next year will be as good.

Government regulation of securities also focuses on making sure openness or transparency occurs. Without the required transparency, management may have a tendency to hide problems, hoping they can be resolved before anyone notices. Failing to take corrective action usually means problems compound. Worst case scenario—some companies eventually face bankruptcy. The collapse often happens so fast, investors can't sell or get out of their holdings, which leads them into losing most if not all of their money. Sometimes the harm is so great it spreads across the entire economy. The bear market of 2008 is an example of a very serious recession caused by the failure of investment houses and insurance companies to keep the public and stockholders fully informed. Government regulation does not completely solve the problem of lack of transparency. Self-preservation and pride leads to finding new ways to conceal problems from the investing public. Management compensation, with a heavy emphasis on performance-based bonuses, encourages corner cutting and high risk decisions to improve quarterly and year-end results.

The investor needs a way to judge whether a company is a risk for a sudden financial surprise that adversely affects its stock. History is an important indicator. If a company has a history of consistent transparency and financial responsibility, this is a good indication that the future, openness and good financial decisions will continue. This does not mean companies that have a clean record cannot have sudden problems. Without answering the safety question, investors cannot pick stocks with a probability information they are using is reliable and safe.

Hunting for an objective measure led me to VectorVest, a computer stock advisory. The founder of VectorVest—Bart Diliddo, PhD—is an engineer by training. He devised a mathematical formula to measure safety called the relative safety index. The index is on a scale of 0.1 to 2.0. The higher the index number the higher the relative safety is. The factors considered when computing the index are earnings consistency, company size, price behavior, longevity, dividend history and debt to equity ratio.

Dr. Diliddo calls safety the missing link. I would agree. I spent hours over many days testing the relative safety index. I discovered, if I compared two stocks with similar earning yield and growth of earning per share—the one with the highest relative safety index number would in the vast majority of time would do better in the future.

A back-test of the year 2000 reveals the effectiveness of the relative safety rating. That year the S&P 500 went down 9.1%. On January 3, 2000, there were 862 stocks with an earnings yield of 10% or greater. The twenty stocks within the 862 stocks with the highest relative safety rating grew 19.0% during the year 2000. The hundred stocks with the highest safety rating grew 13.2%. There is a direct relationship between Dr. Diliddo's relative safety ratings and price growth. In down years it is even more important to pay attention the relative safety rating. Paying attention to safety often makes the difference between poor results and excellent results.

MAKING SENSE OUT OF FINANCIAL STATEMENTS

WITH ALL THE national accounting scandals in recent years, there is a general distrust of company financial reports. Management, accountants and auditors are clever and talented. They use words to get you to think in one way, when in fact the words really mean something else. They are capable of diverting attention away from a serious problem while actually disclosing it. Nonetheless, financial statements tell a very important story to the investor. Whether or not a company is making a profit is a good predictor of how well its stock will do in the stock market. The line items in the financial reports can be important signals that trouble lies ahead. Often trouble can be spotted long before the stock market has noticed. I am surprised by the number of times a financial report has kept me away from a poor-performing stock.

Unfamiliarity and intimidation are the biggest obstacles to overcome when reading a financial statement. Most people have jobs that do not require reviewing the financials of their company. They have little interest in reading them on their own. The view is, why bother when there is not much I can do about it, if trouble is spotted? Plus, whistle blowers are unfavorably looked upon in any business organization. The general attitude is, "If I did read the financial report and it was bad, that would be discouraging, maybe even mind blowing. It is best not to know."

Even small business owners, whose very existence depends upon knowing how well their business is doing, seldom pay attention to their business's financial statements. Many think knowing how much money they have in the bank is good enough. And if trouble arises, they depend on their expense cutting or sales skills to work their way out of trouble. Most small business people prefer to have a positive attitude and not be looking for trouble. I once had a business partner who was great salesperson, but when I tried to review our financial reports with him; he would immediately become frustrated and many times angry in effort to stop me from reviewing them with him. Not reading financials, the business owner could be the last to know their business is going broke. Years ago, I had an accounting teacher who said that if a business owner doesn't pay attention to accounting, it is easy to go bankrupt. By the same token, paying attention to accounting and responding makes it hard not to be successful and nearly impossible to go bankrupt. I have learned over the years if I pay attention to financial reports, I can began to learn to develop performance indicators which will help me monitor my businesses' activities—accurately assessing my businesses' progress. The same is true reviewing companies' financial statements; one begins to have better understanding and sense how financial results affect their stock's performance.

For all the resonance and consternation about financial statements, they are easy to read and understand. Twenty years ago, current financials of publicly held companies were very hard to find. Usually, if an investor did find a company's financial report, it would be a year or more old and of limited value. Today, the Internet has made finding a company's financials fast and easy. An investor can look up the latest financial information by getting onto company websites. I use Yahoo Finance and it is free. Yahoo Finance gives a great summary of most companies' income statement, balance sheet and cash flow statement. Yahoo also does a search of the latest news about each company.

I depend heavily on VectorVest's digital index numbers which describe individual stock characteristics, such as earnings yield, growth of earnings per share and relative safety. You might ask why we need to read financial statements. Stock characteristic index numbers are only as good as the financial statement used to calculate them. An index number is a snapshot taken at a particular point in time. It does not show if a company is improving or declining. If a company is declining, its stock price will fall no matter how good the index number looks.

When a buyer finds a house on sale for $300,000 that looks like every other house in the neighborhood of $500,000 homes, does the bank immediately say go ahead and buy? Or is there a worry something might be seriously wrong with the building? How does the bank find out? It orders an inspection to make sure there are no termites, the floors are not rotted, whether there is insulation in the ceiling and walls, the basement floor is not cracked, there is no evidence of mold or the vacant lot next door isn't zoned for a different use. An investor's search for a stock with value is no different.

An inspection or review of financial statements can often turn up a very serious defect. One looks for red flags warning the investor the stock's value is not what it seems to be. Every investor evaluating financials must ask questions. Try to find the answers. Don't assume what the answer may be. Hunt for hard facts that will answer your question. Make sure it is your mind; not your heart or gut that guides your decision making. When an answer seems to indicate there is trouble, there is one more question: Was the question and answer useful? I once had an instructor who believed the questions asked were more important than telling her what we knew. Curiosity does not kill a cat; it does, however prevent costly mistakes.

Remember the fall of Enron? The stock market was fooled badly. Maybe, if someone had taken the time to study the financials and ask questions, fewer pension and mutual funds would have avoided the embarrassment of taking big write-offs. The sad truth is, red flags could have been found in Enron's financials long before it failed. Either no one bothered to read them with enough scrutiny to spot them, or they didn't want to miss out on what everyone else was doing, so they went with their gut feelings and hoped it wasn't as bad as it seemed to be. Hope can quickly turn into fear without a firm understanding of the factual circumstances. Operating on hope or fear is when mistakes are made. The investor's review of company financials is a pass-fail examination. If an investor sees a red flag, it is important to stop and decide whether to go forward or move onto another stock. It is important to write down your reasoning behind your decision, so later you can go back review and learn if you were right or not.

There are three financial statements prepared from the same information. Each has a purpose. Below are examples of each.

ABC Company
Income Statement

	Year Ending 12/31/10	Year Ending 12/31/09	
Revenue	$1,735,476	$1,509,110	+13.0%
Cost of Revenue	1,391,167	1,148,077	+21.1%
Gross Profit	$ 344,306	$ 361,033	- 4.6%
Expenses:			
Operating Expenses	$ 46,415	$ 42,196	+10.0%
Research and Development	19,450	19,452	0.0%
Selling and Administrative	50,819	44,190	+15.0%
Non-recurring		(17,903)	-100.0%
Interest Expenses	57,940	53,134	+ 9.0%
Depreciation	124,940	112,500	+ 11.1%
Total Expenses	$ 299,564	$ 253,569	+ 18.1%
Net Income	$ 44,745	$ 107,464	- 58.4%

Balance Sheet Year Ending 12/31/10
Year Ending 12/23/09

Current Assets:

Cash	$ 129,385	$ 179,017	-27.7%
Accounts Receivable	266,115	198.791	+33.9%
Inventory	174,581	211,017	-17.3%
Trademark Development	100,000	0	+100%
Total Current Assets	$ 670,081	$ 588,825	+13.7%
Long Term Investments	$ 174,099	$ 164,099	+6.1%
Plant and Equipment	$ 675,957	$ 720,897	-6.2%
Total Assets	$1,520,137	$1,473,821	+3.1%
Current Liabilities:			
Accounts Payable	167,087	$ 232,356	-28.8%
Short-term/Long-term Debt	33,130	33,130	0.0%
Current Liabilities	$ 200,217	$ 265,486	-24.6%
Long Term Debt	$ 298,754	$ 331,300	-9.8%
Employee's Pension Plan	200,000		+100%
Owners' Equity	668,957	768,957	-26.0%
Retained Earnings	152,209	107,464	+41.6%
Total Liabilities and Equity	$1,520,137	$1,473,821	+3.1%

ABC Company
Cash Flow Statement

1/1/2010 Cash Balance	$179,014
Net Income	44,745
Depreciation	129,940
Accounts Receivables	(67,324)
Inventory	36,346
Trademark Development	(100,000)
Long-term Investments	(10,000)
Purchase Plant and Equipment	(80,611)
Accounts Payable	(65,269)
Long-term Debt	(32,546)
Purchase or Sale of Stock	100,000
12/31/2010 Cash Balance	$129,385

THE INCOME STATEMENT

THE INCOME STATEMENT tells the investor the story of the company's revenue, expenses, and net income or profit. The rule should be to invest in a stock whose company has growing revenue and profit, while the cost of revenue and expenses should grow at a lesser rate. Always remember there are over eight thousand stocks. Be picky. Exceptions should be rare and taken seriously.

ABC Company
Income Statement

	Year Ending 12/31/10	Year Ending 12/31/09	
Revenue	$1,735,476	$1,509,110	+13.0%
Cost of Revenue	1,391,167	1,148,077	+21.1%
Gross Profit	$ 344,306	$ 361,033	- 4.6%
Expenses:			
Operating Expenses	$ 46,415	$ 42,196	+10.0%
Research and Development	19,450	19,452	0.0%
Selling and Administrative	50,819	44,190	+15.0%
Non-recurring		(17,903)	-100.0%
Interest Expenses	57,940	53,134	+ 9.0%
Depreciation	124,940	112,500	+ 11.1%
Total Expenses	$ 299,564	$ 253,569	+ 18.1%
Net Income	$ 44,745	$ 107,464	- 58.4%

The first line of the income statement shows the total revenue. Total revenue is the money the company took in from its sales. Both price levels and the ability to pass costs on to customers are determined by the market. As competition for customers increases, it becomes difficult to raise prices. ABC Company's revenue grew 13% while cost of revenue grew 21.1% and total expenses grew 18.1%. These statistics suggest the market is making it tough to raise prices. The possible reasons for this are many and varied. In my experience working with businesses, there is a strong possibility management is not paying attention to their growing costs or they are afraid to raise prices. Either answer suggests management may not be strong as it should be. Competitors may have improved the efficiencies of production capabilities thereby being able to deliver a product more price competitive. ABC's products could be going out of style or have become dated. There are many more possible reasons. You must probe and probe to discover why there is a declining gross profit growth in comparison with both revenue and cost of revenue.

Large changes in sales can be the result of many things, such as, selling off divisions or discontinuing product lines. These changes can be either a good sign or a bad sign. If there was a sell-off of divisions, did the company keep the most profitable or the least profitable? If the company discontinued a product line, what is the new focus of the company? Major companies do change focus. Some example examples include the following: Boise Cascade changed from a lumber company to an office supply company. ITT, in the late 1960's, changed from an international telephone company to one that manufactures and sells paper. A change can transform a run-of-mill operation into something outstanding. Just as likely, a great company can make a real error and turn itself into a complete disaster. As a company changes its mix of business, the income statement can help tell the effect it had on the company's profitability. The challenge for the investor is not try to predict what the effect will be on profitability, but to wait and see the actual effect changes have on the income statement. Patience and waiting for results is the best way to avoid costly mistakes.

The second line of the income statement is the cost of revenue. The cost of revenue is the direct cost to produce the company's products. It is a positive if the cost of revenue is growing at a lesser rate than the growth of the total revenue. Gross profit is calculated by subtracting the cost of revenue from total revenue. The gross profit is called the margin. Growing margins are a good sign. ABC is suffering from a gross profit or margin squeeze. This is not good a good sign.

Subtracting operating expenses, research development, administrative expenses, nonrecurring expenses, and other expenses equals operating net income. Nonrecurring income or expenses can give a false reading of net income. Footnotes do often explain the nonrecurring event. In the year 2009, ABC's nonrecurring expense credit raised net income by $17,903. Financial reports often emphasize nonrecurring items that lower income and put less emphasis on events that enhance net profit.

Management often takes great pride when net operating income grows and sales levels are flat. There is only so much expense cutting that can occur without improving gross sales. The positive net income trend will eventually suffer if over the long term gross sales don't improve. What is the company doing to avoid an eventual net income down turn when it can no longer cut expenses?

Spikes in sales and net operating income should always be questioned. Is the spike a trend or is it a one-time event? Is the spike the result of a new exclusive product? Will competition be able to catch up? Is it the result of an accounting gimmick? Or is it real? Are there other explanations for the spike? If the spike is the beginning of a long term trend, will production become a ceiling that will hamper future growth?

Never quit asking questions. Finding the answer gives the investor an edge and makes him or her much more confident. To find the answers an investor must be willing to read financial reports, competitor financial reports and current news. An investor should be looking for exceptional news that will have a substantial effect on net income; not routine press releases about normal everyday business events. In a fast-moving world always remember annual financial reports become dated quickly. An alert investor also must review quarterly income statements to spot latest trends.

THE BALANCE SHEET

THE BALANCE SHEET is a snapshot of the company's financial condition on a specific day—the last day of a fiscal year or the end of a fiscal quarter. Fiscal years may or may not be the calendar year. The balance sheet shows the company's assets, liabilities and net worth. It is called a balance sheet because assets always equals liabilities and net worth. Current assets are assets that can be readily converted into cash. Current liabilities are bills that must be paid within the next 12 months.

Balance Sheet

	Year Ending 12/31/10	Year Ending 12/23/09	
Current Assets:			
Cash	$ 129,385	$ 179,017	-27.7%
Accounts Receivable	266,115	198.791	+33.9%
Inventory	174,581	211,017	-17.3%
Trademark Development	100,000	0	+100%
Total Current Assets	$ 670,081	$ 588,825	+13.7%
Long Term Investments	$ 174,099	$ 164,099	+6.1%
Plant and Equipment	$ 675,957	$ 720,897	-6.2%
Total Assets	$1,520,137	$1,473,821	+3.1%
Current Liabilities:			
Accounts Payable	$ 167,087	$ 232,356	-28.8%
Short-term/Long-term Debt	33,130	33,130	0.0%
Current Liabilities	$ 200,217	$ 265,486	-24.6%
Long term Debt	$ 298,754	$ 331,300	+9.8%
Employee's Pension Plan	200,000		+100%
Owners' Equity	668,957	768,957	-26.0%
Retained Earnings	152,209	107,464	+41.6%
Total Liabilities and Equity	$1,520,137	$1,473,821	+3.1%

Many business people I deal with do not pay attention to their business's balance sheet. They limit their attention to how much money they have in the bank. If they have a healthy balance that is good enough for them. ABC does have a healthy balance in the bank $129,385. But compare that to last year and it is significantly less. As we look closer ABC's cash position may be even weaker.

A review of the balance sheet can spot possible profitability troubles that will never be found in the income statement. In light of this, special attention should be paid to the accounts receivable and inventory line items. Both can give important signs of impending trouble. ABC's accounts receivable has grown 33.9% while revenue has only grown 13.0%. This is a possible indication that ABC's management has either relaxed their credit standards to get more sales or they have not written off bad debt causing a net profit overstatement which will have to be corrected and written off in the future. Often a new sales manager is hired with marching orders to increase sales. Sales increase, but money is not collected. Sometimes, even worse, it is never tied down when the money will be paid. Sales grow. Profits grow. Accounts receivable grow even faster. The business never has any money to pay bills. The day of reckoning always comes. The company has to record a loss. If the company survives, many times, prior years' income statements will have to be adjusted. The effect is a significate drop in the company's stock price.

Inventory has dropped 17.3%. This may be a sign of more efficient management of the company's inventory. It also may be an indication that management is using inventory reductions to fight off a cash flow problem do to a tightening of credit afforded to the company. Accounts payable have been reduced by $65,269 and long term debt by $32,546. Owner's equity has dropped from $768,957 to $668,957. While the cash flow statement shows $100,000 cash was infused into the business thru the sale of stock. The expectation would be an increase in owner's equity. A new line item Employee Pension Plan was added in amount of $200,000 probably the result of a government audit. None of this activity shows up on the income statement. The balance sheet changes points to serious trouble. Questions have to be asked and answer before investing ABC's stock.

An inventory buildup may be an indication of an accounting problem. A business records the purchase of inventory. But, when the inventory is sold an accounting entry must be made showing a reduction in inventory. Failing to do this will inflate inventory values and reduce expenses, overstating net income.

Even big well know companies have problems overstating inventory. Cisco, a couple of years ago, wrote off a billion dollars because its inventory included a large amount of obsolete products.

Intangible assets include goodwill, patents, and copyrights. These assets are generally deferred expenses recorded as an asset to be written off as an expense over many years. Improperly deferring expenses, recording it as an intangible asset, inflates net income and net worth of the firm. ABC shows a new current asset, trademark development. This raises a red flag. Current assets are assets that can be readily turned into cash. A trademark cannot be sold for cash and word development indicates an expense rather an asset. A likely explanation for recording it as an asset is to avoid a $100,000 expense that would give ABC a $55,258 operating loss rather than a $44,745 net profit. Another sign trouble is brewing.

Current assets should be more than current liabilities. Current assets divided by current liabilities is called the current ratio. Most companies have a goal of having a current ratio of at least 1.5. As discussed, ABC's current assets are overstated by $100,000. Their current assets of $570,081 divided by their current liabilities of $200,217 gives them a current ratio of 2.8.

A debt free company is a real plus. High debt makes the company's profitability vulnerable to interest rates changes and bank loan policies. A friend of mine owned a motorcycle dealership that financed their entire motorcycle inventory. In one summer interest rates went for 8% to 18%. Not only did their interest costs skyrocket; consumer financing became difficult, causing their sales to decline. If their dealership had no debt, it may have been able to weather the storm; instead it went under.

During a time of higher interest rates, debt can become a problem for many retail stocks.

Without a good reason debt growth should never exceed sales growth. If it does it is important to find out why. It can be the result of poor management or it can mean the company is investing in the future.

Stockholders' equity is the amount owners have invested in the business to start it up or expand plus the accumulated profit since it started. It is important that stockholders' equity grows each year. It is surprising how many times "onetime" adjustments show up on the balance sheet that never appear in the income statement. ABC's balance sheet shows such an adjustment. It has added an employee pension plan entry of $200,000. ABC has been underfunding its pension plan and this is a catchup entry covering the failure to record this as an expense in the past. Once noticed, this will cause a drop in its stock price.

Once one starts asking questions, it is amazing how much information can be found in financial reports.

CASH FLOW STATEMENT

THE CASH FLOW statement shows all the sources of cash and where it is spent. It uses the same information as the income statement and balance sheet, but tells the story in a different way. The cash flow statement can be thought of as a summary of the company's checkbook. To survive, a company must have a positive cash flow.

Below is ABC's cash flow statement. The positive numbers show the sources of cash. The negative numbers show where cash was spent.

ABC Company
Cash Flow Statement

1/1/2010 Cash Balance	$179,014
Net Income	44,745
Depreciation	129,940
Accounts Receivables	(67,324)
Inventory	36,346
Trademark Development	(100,000)
Long-term Investments	(10,000)
Purchase Plant and Equipment	(80,611)
Accounts Payable	(65,269)
Long-term Debt	(32,546)
Purchase or Sale of Stock	100,000
12/31/2010 Cash Balance	$129,385

Depreciation is not a cash expenditure, but it is an expense that reduces net income. Since, no cash is spent, $124,940 is added back to the cash balance. Accounts receivable grew $67,324; ABC used cash to finance a larger balance.The smaller inventory added $36,346 to the cash balance. It took $100,000 cash to develop a trademark. ABC spent $10,000 cash for long term investments, $80,611 to purchase plant and equipment, $65,269 to reduce accounts payable, and $32,546 to reduce long-term debt. To raise cash they sold $100,000 stock, thus diluting ownership of the company. The effect is a possible drop in ABC's stock prices.

I have discovered, if I rearrange the cash flow statement to the following, it is much easier to comprehend:

1/1/2010 Cash Balance		$179,014
Sources of Cash:		
Net Income	$ 44,745	
Depreciation	124,940	
Inventory reduction	36,436	
Sale of Stock	100,000	
Total Sources of Cash		$306,121
Uses of Cash:		
Growth of Accounts Receivable	$ 67,324	
Trademark Development	100,000	
Purchase of Plant and Equipment	80,611	
Purchase of Long Term Investments	10,000	
Reduction of Accounts Payable	65,269	
Reduction of Long Term Debt	32,546	
Total Uses of Cash		$355,750
12/31/2010 Cash Balance		$129,385

THE FINANCIAL REPORT CHECK LIST

HERE IS A financial check list with the correct answers. Circle the answers shown that apply to the stock you are considering.

1. Are sales growing every year? Yes
2. Is the cost of sales growing at the same rate or lesser than sales? Yes
3. Is the net profit growing at the same rate or greater than sales? Yes
4. Has the company's line of business remained the same? Yes
5. Has the company had any non-recurring income or expenses? No
6. Is there a spike in income or expenses? No
7. Are accounts receivable growing faster than sales? No
8. Is inventory growing faster than sales? No
9. Are any pre-paid expenses recorded as an asset? No
10. Is the company debt free? Yes
11. Is the current ratio more than 1.5? Yes
12. Is the company buying back their stock? Yes
13. Is the owners' equity growing every year? Yes

The more answers that are circled, the better the stock may be.

THE CASH PROBLEMS

INSTEAD OF BEING cash poor, companies can have an opposite problem—too much cash. A buildup of excessive amounts of cash can pose both advantages and problems for companies. Cash rich companies have three choices to avoid having some other company find it profitable to take them over.

The first choice is to buy their company's stock. The stockholders benefit from the extra demand for the stock, causing the price of the stock to rise. The three years before Safeco Insurance was purchased by Liberty Mutual Insurance Company, Safeco had little total revenue growth, they had excessive amounts of cash. Safeco began purchasing their own stock—more than $1.9 billion worth, these purchases represented nearly a third of their outstanding stock. The effect on earnings per share was significant, causing Safeco stock prices to triple.

The second choice is to increase dividends. For example, several years ago, Microsoft gave a large onetime cash dividend to stockholders.

The third choice is to buy other companies. Companies with a lot of cash can get sloppy and overpay. Also, the management of a successful company can become overconfident and bold. They believe they can run every business just as well as they are running the company they presently are managing. They fail to recognize their success can be the result of a culture of excellence in their company that has built up over years and less to do with the management at the very top. While they may be good managers, they may not be as successful at another company because it does not have the same culture. They buy such a company with cash or their stock. A problem is only detected after the purchase. A good example is when Safeco Insurance Company purchased American States Insurance Company from Lincoln National Insurance. It was only after the deal was completed that Safeco discovered American States had a history of under-reserving claims. This meant there was not enough money set aside to settle claims. When all the problems were resolved, Safeco was the same size it was it was before it purchased American States.

The rule of thumb is, the stock of the company being acquired will rise. The stock of the acquiring company will fall. When a company starts buying other companies, you need to ask, can I do a better job? Unless this is a company with a successful history of acquiring companies, often you can do a better job picking stock. Then selling the acquiring company's stock and finding another company's stock is a good choice.

Some companies particularly companies that are either starting up or growing very fast don't have a lot of cash. The management of these companies pays themselves and their employees in stock rather than cash. If they do this at a faster rate than the growth of net income, the value of the stock will decline causing the price of its stock to decline. There is, however, an advantage when employees own stock. They have an interest in making certain the company is both profitable and growing.

THE WORLD ECONOMY

W E ARE RAPIDLY becoming a part of a World economy. More and more foreign stocks are being traded on American stock exchanges. Increasingly American companies are moving their operations outside of the United States. United States tax laws provide an incentive to move their operations and jobs overseas. U.S. corporations do not have to pay income taxes on overseas profits until the money from profits is actually brought back in the United States.

There is a great debate about the effectiveness of foreign regulations on products and financial reporting. Most countries have high standards, but there is a worry about other countries. Many countries have gone to the extreme in deregulating their economies. Eastern European and Russian economies went from being totally controlled by their governments to being nearly totally unregulated. If you are politically conservative, you might be inclined to say, "What is wrong with that?" As a matter of fact, a totally free market with no regulations has a history of rewarding dishonest behavior over honest behavior. Without government regulations or criminal penalties, management in an effort to be competitive are tempted to cut corners, participate in fraud, adapt improper accounting methods and hide financial problems. Often what seems to be a fast-growing, profitable company is actually a criminal enterprise. Problems for the investor is these companies at some point refuse to abide by American regulations causing their stock to be delisted on American stock exchanges. The lack of safety regulations lead to the selling of defective products. When this is discovered it can bankrupt a company.

The lesson I have learned living in Yakima, Washington is my ability to have firsthand knowledge about foreign countries and the effect of their regulations is practically nil. I have two defenses. I need to pay attention to the news with special attention to being able to spot problems. I need to diversify my investments and avoid putting too many eggs from one country into my basket.

THE COST OF MONEY: THE BASIS OF VALUE

THE COMMON WISDOM seems to be the earnings yield of a stock should be at least two percentage points greater that the interest rates of an AAA corporate bond. The risk of ownership is greater than the risk of owning a bond. This increase of risk should be rewarded. If a company should fail and its assets are sold, the proceeds of the sale first goes to paying off the secured creditors. If there is any money left, then the general or unsecured creditors are paid off, next in line are the preferred stockholders and last in line are the common stockholders.

I have found common wisdom does not seem to apply to the stocks I own. Historically my stocks have a sell off point when their earnings yield becomes less than an average of 4.29 percentage points above the composite corporate bond rate. As I am writing this the corporate bond rate is 4.31%. This means when the earnings yield of the stocks I own approaches 8.6%, selling time has arrived. All stocks are not alike. My stocks historically have historical selling earnings yields that range from 5.49% to 10.73%. Presently, I use 8.6% earnings yield as a guide to sell, unless its selling point seems to have a higher earnings yield (these percentages change as interest rates change).

To lessen the confusion below are some examples using earnings per share and corporate bond interest rates of 4.31% plus 4.29% or 8.6% to value stocks as to when to buy and when to sell:

First example: I am trying to decide whether to buy. The stock price is $37.89. Its earnings per share is $1.90. The value of the stock would be $1.90 divided by 8.6% or $22.09. The $22.09 value of this stock is less than its price of $37.89. This stock is a poor buy.

Second example: I am trying decide whether to buy. The stock price is $19.20. The earnings per share is $4.87. The value of the stock is $4.87 divided by 8.6% or $56.63. The $56.63 value is more than the stock price of $19.20. This company would be a great candidate to add to your portfolio.

Third example: Let's make this example a little more complex. The company makes horse buggies. This is not an expanding industry. The company's stock closed at $15.80 on low volume. This last year the price range of the stock was a low of $14.85 with a high of $35.15. Its earnings per share are $4.18 and it has been near amount for nearly fifteen years. Should we buy this stock tomorrow?

The earnings yield of this stock when the stock is at its highest price is $4.18 divided by $35.18 or 11.88%. The market has determined the risk reward for owning this stock is 11.88% minus the corporate bond rate of 4.31% or 7.57%. The value of this stock is 4.18% divided by 11.88% or $35.15. At $14.85 it is an excellent buy. Until this stock's price begins to move, not a lot of analysts will be writing about it. Horse buggies were hot sellers two centuries ago, they are not today. Analysts are drawn to high-tech, fast growing companies whose stock prices are thirty to fifty times earnings. High-tech has lure of exciting new products, ideas, and unrealized potential of big profits in the future. There is a snowball effect, as it keeps rolling the excitement and the popularity of a high-tech stock keeps growing. However, these popular companies often do disappoint causing complaints that playing the stock market is merely casino gambling. High-tech companies often only offer hope not a solid history of earnings.

The earnings history of this horse-buggy stock indicates that there is a good chance this stock's price will grow more than a 100% this next year. Past investors of this stock will take notice of its low price and will start buying it. The risk/reward ratio is very favorable. Today we should buy the horse buggy stock.

Let's jump to one year from now. Its stock price is $37.92. As result of the company finding a new product to sell, its earnings per share has risen from $4.18 to $6.15. Should we be selling? The stock's value is $6.15 by 11.88% or $51.77. Even though this horse buggy stock has gone past its previous high of $35.18 it is still a good stock to hold onto.

Using earnings yields is a very effective guide. However, earnings yield information is not available in newspapers, business journals, over the radio or TV. Your neighbors will not know what you are talking about. Nonetheless, this information can be at your fingertips in just a few seconds. You do have to have a computer and stock analysis software.

COMPARE WITH OTHER COMPANIES

EVEN THOUGH I never played baseball in my younger years, I consider baseball as my favorite sport. It is a game of match ups. Every batter, pitcher and fielder has their strengths and weaknesses. They can be statistically measured. To get better results teams can drill down through the statistics and strategies are developed to exploit both strengths and weaknesses. Every game depending on who is playing a strategy is developed matching of strengths to strengths, or strengths to weaknesses, or weaknesses to weaknesses.

The same can be done as we begin to understand the relationships between earnings yields, growth of earnings per share, safety from adverse surprises and market pricing of risks. There are times when the market places emphasis on earnings yields, other times the emphasis may be on growth or safety. Comparing similar companies can lead to better investment choices. I use Yahoo Finance, Fidelity Finance and VectorVest to do my comparisons. Each uses a difference perspective which are very helpful. Until a comparison is completed, you cannot be sure you have selected the most promising company within an industry.

For me VectorVest has the most useful chart. They actually compare all of the companies within an industry group. The chart shows earnings yield, growth of earnings per share and safety. It makes easy to spot strengths and weaknesses of each of these areas. One can design stock charts showing all the relevant characteristics you deem as applicable. I use stock prices, ten, twenty and forty day moving averages, timing and earning yields on my chart. You can click on the previous points where the stock has dropped, it will show the exact date of the drop. VectorVest has history chart that will show the earnings yield, growth of the earnings per share, safety ratings and earnings yield for that day. From this information you can began to form opinions which stock is a better fit for your portfolio. A stock within a growing or leading industry has the potential to do better than a stock in a stable or languishing industry. What seems at first to be a good choice before a comparison can lead to a better choice after the comparison.

Business news can provide an investor with useful information. There are two kinds of news. One is announcements of routine business dealings. These are generally of no value. The other are announcements of significant changes in the business operations, in the law and the economy. It is imperative not to take just one story at its face value. There needs to be a vigorous checking of each story that seems to have a significant impact on the company or industry. An example would be several years ago there was a government crackdown on private colleges that had poor graduation and job placement results. This resulted in substantial drop in stock prices of private for profit colleges. In fact, several for profit colleges were forced into bankruptcy as a result of this legislation.

Self-evaluation does improve decision making. A written record of your thought processes that go into your decision making is essential. Your comments need to cover your objective observations concerning earnings, growth and safety. Also, you need to record your instinctive thinking, which so many times overpowers objective observations. Particularly, the feelings surrounding your impulses to sell a particular stock. A review of your writings will give you better understanding of your decision making process and the emotions that drives your decisions. Unfortunately, it is not reality but emotions and false assumptions about reality that creeps into your mind and drives decision making. The review will become a great learning tool. Much can be learned from both your failures and successes.

BACK-TESTING: PROOF IT WORKS

THE PROOF IS in the pudding. Our strategy is to pay attention to relevant information. This will lead to a better decisions. I have argued that earnings yield, growth of earnings per share, safety and the cost of money are the important characteristics of a successful stock market strategy. It is all unproven theory until it has been tested in the marketplace. The answer to whether the theory will work or not, can only be answered by stock market experience.

Investors can gain experience in two ways. One is to be in the market actually buying and selling stocks. This will take a long time in the market before being able to determine if a theory works. The downside of learning by trial and error is that the mistakes can be very expensive. Losing money can make it easy to become discouraged and give up.

The other alternative to gain experience is by back-testing. Back-testing is defined as using historical data to test how an investment strategy would have fared in the past. The idea is to find out what works and what does not work without putting money on the line. The hypothesis is, if a strategy works well in the past, it will work well in the future. Through back-testing you can gain the knowledge and confidence that will lead to effective investing.

Stock prices do not move up or down in a steady, straight line in the stock market. Stock prices move in waves, peaks and valleys. Whatever direction the stock price is moving for just a few days, it is human nature to assume this will continue far into the future. If a stock suffers a drop in price, a normal reaction is to act as if the price will be going down forever. A less than confident investor will often act, forgetting to check whether or not the reasons for buying the stock still exist. Panic often cause one to act contrary to their best interests. Only by becoming familiar with market behavior can the investor gain the perspective and confidence to make the right decisions.

Back-testing has one hazard; the tester already knows the past. This knowledge can contaminate a back-test. The tester must pay attention to the influence of his or her historical knowledge so it will not affect the back-test. Letting your historical knowledge have influence can rig the back-test, causing an investor to make false assumptions.

The elements of a good back-test include a defined investment strategy conducted over a set time frame which should include at least both a bull and bear market. The returns should be annualized and percentages should be converted into dollar amounts. That way profit and losses can be determined. The back-test should be measured against a bench mark.

THE BACK-TEST

THE TIME HAS come when it is necessary to have the right tools, a computer and with back-testing software. VectorVest's "Unisearch" application will be able to back-test using the stock characteristics—earnings yield, growth of earnings per share and safety—as effective predictors. The name of the back-test will be called, High Quality Stocks. It will have the following characteristics:

1. An earnings yield of at least 10%.
2. An earnings per share growth of at least 10%.
3. A VectorVest safety rating of at least 0.95.
4. A stock price of $25 or less.

The High Quality Stock test will cover a ten year period of time beginning January 3, 2000 and ending January 4, 2010. (I am using a random ten year period because I do not want my knowledge of how stock did during a specific period as this could contaminate the test.)

A. Each year, twenty-five stocks will be selected from the universe of stocks defined above. The stocks in the universe will be ranked by their PEG rating. The top twenty-five stock winners and losers will be noted.
B. A twenty-five thousand dollar investment will be made on January 3, 2000 and it will be sold on the second trading day of the following year. The principal and the profit will be reinvested the following year.
C. The results of the High Quality Stock back-test will be measured against the results of the S&P 500.

To understand how a back-test selects the stocks and records its results, it is important to go through each step of the back-test.

1. Access the universe of 8,067 stocks that are available in the stock market on January 3, 2000.

2. Eliminate stocks with a price above $25. This leaves 2,270 stocks in the universe.

3. Eliminate from the 2,270 stocks all the stocks that fail to have a growth rate of 10%. This leaves 939 stocks in the universe.

4. Eliminate from the 939 all stocks that do not have a relative safety rating of 0.95. This leaves 335 stocks in the universe.

5. Eliminate from the 335 all stocks that do not have an earnings yield of at least 10%. This leaves a final universe of 123 stocks.

6. Rank the remaining 123 stocks by their PEGs, from the best to the worst.

7. Select the twenty-five stocks with the best PEGs for the year 2000 back-test.

8. Run the 2000 back-test. The back-test results show fifteen stocks that registered a gain and ten stocks that recorded a loss. The twenty-five stock universe showed a 26.4% gain. If $1,000 had been invested in each of the twenty-five stocks. The $25,000 would have grown to $31,600 by January 4, 2001. On January 4, 2001 the entire $31,600 will be invested in the twenty-five stocks selected for the year 2001.

9. This process will be repeated for each year through the end of 2009. VectorVest's Unisearch application will calculate the gain or loss of each twenty-five stock universe including the results of each stock within each universe.

Chart #1 Section #1, on the next page shows the results of the back-test for each of the ten years. The first column is the year of the back-test.

The second column shows the percentage of growth of the S&P 500 for the year. Christopher H. Browne points out that 85% of professional portfolio managers fail to beat the S&P 500.

The third column shows the number of stocks in the universe from which the final selection of twenty-five stocks was made.

The fourth column shows the percentage gain or loss.

The last column shows the number of winners and losers.

Section #2 of Chart #1 translates the results into dollar amounts to illustrate the profit and loss of the High Quality Stock back-test.

Chart #1 Section #1

Year	S&P 500 Growth	Number of Stocks in HQS Universe	High Quality Stocks Back-test results	Winners/Losers
2000	-9.1%	124	+ 26.4%	15/10
2001	-11.9%	117	+ 55.5%	20/5
2002	-22.1%	50	+ 8.0%	16/9
2003	+28.7%	102	+120.6%	24/1
2004	+10.9%	39	+ 46.8%	17/8
2005	+ 4.9%	35	+ 39.6%	17/8
2006	+12.0%	85	+ 24.6%	15/10
2007	+ 0.9%	54	+ 5.5%	10/15
2008	-42.2%	68	- 45.5%	3/22
2009	+29.9%	73	+ 75.8%	24/1
Ave.	+ 0.2%	74.7	+ 35.7%	16/9

Chart #1 Section #2—Converting section #1's results into dollars.

Year	S&P 500	High Quality Stocks
January 2000	$25,000	$ 25,000
January 2001	22,457	31,600
January 2002	19,800	49,138
January 2003	15,424	53,069
January 2004	20,031	117,070
January 2005	22,214	171,858
January 2006	23,302	239,858
January 2007	26,098	298,934
January 2008	27,223	315,376
January 2009	15,734	171,879
January 2010	20,372	302,165
Net Gain/Loss	$ -4,625	$277,164

It is worth pointing out the average annual growth percentage is 35.7% that averages out to be less than 3% a month. Thirty-five percent average annual growth over a ten year period is considered outstanding by anyone's judgment. I am one who cannot resist seeing every day how well I did in the stock market. I have to remind myself constantly day to day fluctuations are nearly meaningless.

IS THERE ROOM FOR IMPROVEMENT?

THE BACK-TEST RESULTS need to be analyzed. The first question is does the back-test work? Secondly, can the results be improved upon? The test covered times when the market was both bearish and bullish. The High Quality Stocks did better than the S&P 500 during both times. The back-test did slightly worse than the S&P 500 when the market experienced the severe drop in 2008.

During the ten years, the S&P recorded a net loss of 18.5%. While High Quality Stocks recorded a gain of 1,108%. Translating this into a dollar comparison High Quality Stocks grew from $25,000 to $277,164 while the S&P 500 lost $4,628. Consistency is important High Quality Stocks recorded a profit 9 out of 10 years. The S&P 500 recorded losses four of the ten years.

There is room for improvement. In spite of the overall picking success of High Quality Stock back-test, thirty-six percent of the stocks picked were losers. To reduce the number of losers, it is important to discover the common characteristics of the losing stocks. We should only consider characteristics that can be measured objectively. Stock market success is directly related to the ability to make unemotional decisions. VectorVest has a number of stock characteristics built into their software. Reviewing them is most helpful. Over the years, it is important to keep a diary noting some of common characteristics losing stocks have.

When picking stocks, it is not only important to consider today's earnings yield, but also it is important to pay attention to the stock's historical earnings yields. I go to VectorVest's stock's stock chart to determine the last two dates when a significate price drop of the stock occurred. I look up the stock's earnings yields of the stock on those two dates (which are available on VectorVest's stock analysis page). If today's earnings yield of the stock is not 25% greater than earnings yield of stock when its price last dropped, I do not buy the stock. If I do buy the stock I continue to use the two price drop earnings yields. As its price rises, I hold the stock until its earnings yield drops to the earnings yield level when the stock last fell. If the stock's price does not rise, but its earnings yield falls—I sell the stock.

I have discovered a better time to buy stocks is when the stock market is down. However, I wait to buy an individual stock until its price is higher than it was five trading days ago. As the stock market is peaking it is a poorer time to buy a stock.

If institutional ownership is thirty percent or higher the stock has a higher probability of success. I also have discovered stocks that have an institutional ownership exceeding 100% do poorly.

Paying attention to general market news is helpful. Most of the times the market overacts causing both rises and falls in stock prices. Other times there are important political or economic news that will foretell a rise or fall in stock prices. Examples of this is when changes occurred in government student loan policies "for profit" colleges suffer lower enrollments and lower profits. In fact, several were forced into bankruptcy. Rising interest rates can affect real estate companies' profits causing their stock to fall.

I cannot emphasize enough how important it is to keep a written diary reflecting the day's news with your interpretation of the significance it may have on your stocks. It is important to improve your ability to spot significant news before the stock market reacts.

Business news writers and commentators let their political and other biases subjectively influence their thinking. They also have tendency to write what they think you want to hear instead of what you need to hear and know. They have a real important profit motive to expand readership and listenership. Reality often takes a back seat. No matter what, it is up to us to dig deeper and question what we are hearing or reading. The writers and commentators have a tendency to over-react to news and misinterpret its significance— causing the market to over-react or under-react. Seldom do writers and commentators accurately predict the really big market collapses or how long a market might rise.

The goal I have set for myself is to develop a sense of market rhythms and to see reality. I want to trust my judgment and not be influenced by groupthink. The best example of destructive groupthink is told by one my favorite authors, Damon Runyon.

BAD DAY AT THE HORSE RACES

DAMON RUNYON WROTE this short story in the 1930's. (I am paraphrasing as I need to confess I can't remember the exact names he used in telling this story.)

Eddie lived next to a horse farm. He loved to watch the horses train. Every day he would watch and listen to the trainers rave about a young colt named Lemon Drop. He realized this was his opportunity to win big money when Lemon drop would run in his first race. Then and there Eddie decided that is when he would make his big bet. Except, Eddie didn't have any money to spare. So, he made an extreme effort to cut back on his expenses and save. Over the next several months with a great deal of sacrifice he saved a $1,000 dollars.

Race day came for Lemon Drop to make his debut. Eddie caught the first train to the track. He did not want anything to go wrong that would prevent him from making his bet. Eddie arrived at the track early. The odds on Lemon Drop were fifty to one. No one else knew about Lemon Drop. This would be the day Eddie would turn a thousand dollars into fifty thousand dollars.

As Lemon Drop's race drew near, Eddie stood in line to make his bet. As he listened, no one was betting on Lemon Drop. Eddie begin to have his doubts. He started to think about all the effort it took to save up a thousand dollars. A horse named Duffy's Pride was the betting favorite. A well-dressed man ahead of him bet two thousand dollars on Duffy's Pride. Eddie looked at the Racing Form showing Duffy's Pride's times. Duffy's Pride was indeed a very fast horse. Superstitions began to creep into his mind. The word Lemon could a very bad sign. Eddie began to think, what if he was wrong and lose all his money. He moved to the betting window, Eddie paused, thought about it, then said, "A thousand to win on Duffy's Pride."

The race went off. Duffy's Pride immediately went to the lead. Lemon Drop fell into last place. Eddie was relieved he had at the last second to have the good sense to change his mind. Then, as the horses came down the stretch toward the finish line, Lemon Drop began to pass horses. Just at the finish line Lemon Drop put his nose ahead of Duffy's Pride and won the race. Eddie lost all his money.

Groupthink did Eddie in. What happened to Eddie too many times happens to an investor. Hearing or reading, "You can't miss with this stock, or Warren Buffett has thousands of shares of this stock." There is no proof he actually did. Many times a well written mailer with six, seven or eight pages of fluff with no actual financial information arrives to your home. Newspapers and television programs are always touting stocks, encouraging us to buy. We actually buy and the stock drops we panic and sell.

Objective information should always be at the root of the decision-making process. Eddie did not even trust himself enough to give equal consideration to his very good information about the horse. He could have hedged his bet and split the money on both horses. But, he didn't. Instead all his efforts went for naught. Groupthink was just too powerful. You can never be consistently successful until you believe in what you have learned.

ARE THERE BETTER TIMES TO BUY OR SELL?

O VER THE YEARS of keeping track of my buys and sells, I have learn to pay attention to the following generalizations. They are not hard and fast rules, but I do have to have some very important reasons for not paying attention to them.

1. Buy when the value is more than the price.
2. Sell when the price approaches the value.
3. ***The better time to buy is when the market is bottoming out.*** It is very tempting to buy when the market is peaking. Have patience and wait for the next down turn. There are times, it seems every stock I buy does not do as well as I expected. Invariably, when I go back and review why I didn't do as good as expected, I discovered, I am buying when the market is nearing or right at a peak. I cannot emphasize enough when a market peaks; it is a bad time to buy any stock. VectorVest has a market timing index. As a rule of thumb I usually find better buys when the index is below 1.0.
4. Pay attention to institutional buying and ownership. I try to buy stocks that have at least 30% institutional ownership. There are two reasons institutional ownership is important. The first has to do with the laws of supply and demand. As institutional ownership increases, there is less stock available to buy. One has to pay more for the stock to induce the remaining owners to sell their stock. Less stock available puts pressure to move prices upward. Secondly, institutions have resources to conduct extensive research. Institutional ownership is an important validation of the conclusions I came to after doing my due diligence. Information about both institutional buying and ownership can be found on Yahoo Finance. I use Fidelity Investments as my online broker. Fidelity also offers this

information on their website. It is important to never allow institutional ownership to override one's decision that a stock is too risky to buy.

5. Decisions to buy should be based upon objective data: earnings per share, growth of earnings per share and safety. If any of these become unfavorable, it is time to sell. Most of the time this happens long before the stock price begins to fall. Selling too soon is far more profitable than selling too late.

6. Do not buy stock with short selling that exceeds 10% of the outstanding stock. Short sellers borrow stocks and then sell the stock. Short sellers must buy back the stock before the end of the following year. It is important to remember short sellers are smart and they know what they are doing. Secondly, I review the stocks I own to make sure there has not been significant increase in short selling. If this happens selling the stock is good idea.

All of this is easy to say. Sticking to the rules is hard to do, particularly when it is my money that is on the line. Without a firm foundation based on objective data, it is easy to lose the discipline needed to be successful. As the market makes it normal dips and sell-offs, the urge to sell can be overwhelming, in spite of very favorable earnings and growth. The flip side seeing popular stocks with little or no earnings rise can stir an uncontrollable urge to buy. Discipline is a learned and necessary trait to have in order to be successful.

TEMPTATIONS CAN RUIN THE BEST-LAID PLANS

AN INVESTOR IS constantly tempted to ignore objective information and go with popular subjective pressures. When temptations take over good decision making plummets. Here is my list of temptations I have had to guard against.

Temptation 1: Buy-Sell-Hold Lists. Financial newspapers, business cable channels, analyst newsletters and friendly neighborhood investment brokers all have their recommendations. It is easy to assume they know more than us. The reality is "Buys" often disappoint. Popularity, not value, often determines when a stock makes the Buy list. The inclination is to buy a highly recommended stock without looking at its earnings per share, growth of earning per share or safety. It used to be, I would pay attention to the "experts" and buy their recommended stocks. Then I would watch the same stocks drop in price, panic and sell when the stock was nearing its low. This was story of my investing career. I have learned over the years "Hold" and "Sell" stocks consistently outperform "Buy" stocks. The idea is to look for hold or sell stocks with mediocre looking charts that represent healthy companies. If a stock has value and has no adverse news about its operation, don't be afraid of buying it. It can be a real gem, particularly if the stock has a history of higher prices.

Temptation 2: Highly Popular Stocks. It is exciting to read about a stock that has gone up continuously for the last few years. Popularity is often confused with value. People like to talk about their successes. This adds to the popularity of a stock. Popular stocks do attract investors. Stock analysts hunt for stocks that will be appealing to their readers. Stocks with rising prices seem to be emphasized in their newsletters. It is safer to write about them, particularly if others are doing it also. How can a writer be singled out for making a mistake if everyone else is making the same mistake? This does not get around the fact they are often wrong. If a stock is featured in a magazine, financial newsletter or television show, it is probably too late for you to buy the stock. As is often said, "The train has left the station." Instead of paying attention to hype, time is better spent putting the focus on current earnings and growth. Take the guesswork out of the decision making process by staying on solid ground of limiting your choices to stocks with excellent earnings yields, growth of earnings per share and safety. That is why VectorVest's stock picking has become so important in my success. It enables me to search for and find stocks with characteristics I consider to be important.

Temptation 3: Financial Newsletters. All the time, I get mail touting a financial newsletter. The "financial analyst" brags about finding a penny stock that has grown a 1,000% this last year. If one makes fifty recommendations and one of those recommendations makes it, it is that stock the financial advisor singles out to prove their brilliance. Newsletter writers are selling their opinions. They seldom miss an opportunity to brag. All I can say if you choose to subscribe is never forget about the importance of value. If a stock lacks the financials showing it is making a profit, forget the stock—no matter how enticing the story may be.

Temptation 4: Stocks that are jumping in today's market. Making decisions based solely on price momentum is nothing more than casino type gambling. Years ago, Helen and I learned this lesson in few hours while sitting in a Las Vegas hotel. We had a few minutes to spare, so we started watching CNBC. One stock started to appear many times on the stock ticker at the bottom of the television screen. Each time it appeared its price was higher and higher. After watching this for a few minutes, Helen could not resist. She brought $10,000 worth of this stock. In just a few minutes the stock was worth $20,000, then $30,000 onto $40,000. The CEO of the company appeared on TV, saying he had no idea why buyers were buying and driving the price up. Within an hour Helen was up $50,000.

DONALD L. HINMAN

Helen, who is much better gambler than me wanted to sell. I was hooked by the upward momentum, had caught the exciting fever which greatly fueled my emotions. I said, "Let's hang on for a little while longer." Then, suddenly, the price began to drop like a rock. Helen had the good sense to sell immediately. Luckily, we got out with a $25,000 profit. You would think Helen would talk about the day we made $25,000 just sitting in a Las Vegas hotel room. But all she has been able to do over the years is to tell everybody I refused to listen to her and caused us to lose $25,000.

The lesson learned from this experience is; it was not the financial information that drove the price up and then drove it down even faster. Hopefully, it was not fraud that caused the action that day. More likely, it was caused by people like Helen and I watching CNBC, seeing the rapid price movement going up as the stock ticker went across the TV screen. The stock became very enticing, so we all jumped in immediately and brought the stock. The stock's sudden and surprising popularity was irresistible. Just as sudden, the investors came to their senses, like my Helen, began to say this is too good to be true and started to sell in bunches. The stock suddenly became unpopular. No one likes to hang out with phony people. Stocks with phony prices are treated the same way. As we learn in life, phonies can be very popular for a while; but once they are discovered to be less than they first appear, they lose their popularity.

When the whole stock market is going up, it is very hard not to pick a winner. When the market is going down, it seems every stock suffers a price reduction. It is easy to become discouraged and stay out of the market too long and miss the early stages of the up market, when stock prices surge upwards. When the market is down is the best time to hunt and find stocks with value that is much more than their price.

Temptation 5: Paying attention only to a stock chart's upward price momentum. It is a real temptation to only pay attention to price movements when viewing a stock chart. Extending the price movement alone out into the future can lead to real trouble. Trading volume coupled with price movement can give a clearer picture what may happen in the future. As a stock price peaks in the past it is important to know the stock's earnings yield on those dates. One can use earnings yield history when estimating the probabilities of price growth and when its price may drop. More on stock charts will be covered in the next chapter.

Temptation 6: Trying to guess when sell-offs may occur. Every year seems to have regular times when the market suffers a sell-off. September and October is one of the sell-off times. There is never an exact date or week we can point out and definitely say this is when a sell-off will occur in the future. There is a real temptation to guess and try to be out of the market when general stock market prices fall. The market also experiences a sudden rebound in September and October. If an investor is out of the market when prices fall and then stays out too long when the rebound occurs there will be substantial loss of opportunity to make a profit. Instead of trying to guess when a sell-off or rebound may occur, stay in the market. It is better to base your decisions on a stock's value and safety.

Temptation 7: Buying stock on the margin. When the market is going up, there is a real temptation to leverage results by borrowing money from your broker to buy additional stocks. This is called buying on the margin. The Federal Reserve sets the margin loan requirements. As I write this, the margin requirement is 50%. This means the margin loan cannot be more than 50% of the stocks one owns. If the loan exceeds 50% the investor has to add cash to the brokerage account or sell stocks to reduce the debt below 50%. When this happens, it is called a margin call. When I do VectorVest back-testing I am often tempted to only use year to year time frames. A closer month to month or even shorter time back-test, one will quickly discover the price trends never move in straight line. There are peaks and valleys throughout the year. If a stock portfolio is fully invested using margin loans during up periods one will experience more profits.

In a downturn losses will accelerate sometimes forcing a margin call. Even if there is not a margin call, having a margin loan will increase pressure to sell making it hard to stay the course. I want my decisions to be based on value not market price pressure that might cause me to panic. For certain, I do not want a margin call to be the basis for selling. I have learned if I want to avoid my emotions taking over, I need to avoid as much as possible buying stock on the margin.

Temptation 8: Putting your eggs in one basket. Every so often, there is a stock that sizzles for a prolonged period of time. The temptation is to buy a lot more of that stock. There are also many stocks that appear to be the next sizzler but fizzle out. It is easy to be fooled. Small investors don't have the resources to tell the difference. (Quite frankly I don't think large institutional investors with all their resources can do much better.) One of my past bosses pointed out, if you look at gray horses long enough, you will start to have a hard time telling which horses are white which are black. The defense against taking huge losses caused by one stock is to diversify. Don't put all your eggs or stocks in one basket.

Risk must be spread over many stocks and industries. This will improve your odds for success. Warren Buffett reminds us the market is both a voting machine measuring popularity and a weighing machine measuring value. Popularity is often short term. Value is long term. Looking a value stock's unremarkable price chart and buying it can often be counter-intuitive. A popular stock can be very enticing, the stock's rising price can tempt an investor to load up their portfolio buying it and becoming at risk of losing big.

Remember to follow these simple and easy rules:

1. Buy when value is more than price.
2. When the market is down, there are more buying opportunities.
3. When deciding which stocks to buy put a priority on stocks with increasing institutional buying and ownership.
4. Pay attention to short selling.
5. Sell when value approaches price.
6. Keep yourself away from buying stock on the margin or least keep margin buying to a minimum.

7. Diversify. Don't put all your eggs in one basket.

List the temptations that has lured your decision-making away from being based on objective observations of financial data measuring the characteristics you determine a stock must have before buying or selling it.

DONALD L. HINMAN

ZEROING IN: CHARTS AND INDEX NUMBERS

LARGE AND SMALL investors read stock charts for the same reason—they want to time their buys and sells to maximize their profits. There is also a big difference. Big investors worry about the effect their buying and selling has on a stock's price. They want to buy without driving the price up, and sell without driving the price down. The temptation to illegally manipulate stock prices lies just under the surface. With regularity it seems someone gets arrested. The line between what is legal and illegal is blurred. Being manipulated by someone else's action is always a worry. This makes the argument buying and selling should be based on value.

Unlike the big buyer, the small buyer trades in very small quantities and pays no attention to the effect they have on the market. The small investor reads stock charts to take advantage of price movements. Until you are convinced reading charts work for you, my advice is, don't use them. Stock charts can drive the nonprofessional over the edge and out of the stock market.

When I began reading the stock charts, I did not find them useful. I used them to try to predict the future. I could not do it, mainly because I paid no attention to value. I read several books, trying to learn classic patterns that would indicate what the future may be. The authors claimed there were certain patterns that would be good indicators of a stock's propensity to rise or fall. I found them to not work as advertised. I gave up trying to read stock charts and instead chose to go with what professional chart readers predicted. Finding a current analysis of a stock chart was nearly impossible. When I did find one, more often than not, the written analysis was cleverly hedged and of limited value.

Charts do give an excellent visual of the historical record of prices. I could never get out of my mind that mastering stock charts could be very important. A stock chart clearly shows what the market has done. I wanted better insight and kept up my hunt for insight, I believed that would improve my investing skills. For a very long time I could not find a use for stock charts that would be helpful. And I became convinced the average do-it-yourself investor could never actually benefit from reading a stock chart. I concluded, charts were probably an effective sales tool for a salesman who knew how to construct a sales pitch around them. But for me as an investor, they had no real value.

Then I learned the concepts of divergence and contradiction. A divergence occurs when two chart indicators are going in the opposite direction. For instance, the stock price is going up and its trading volume is dropping, indicating a possible future price drop.

A contradiction occurs when pieces of information are giving conflicting indications. An example of a contradiction is when the price of a stock is flat and at the same time, the stock has a high earnings yield and a history of continuous earning per share growth. A flat price line shows buyer and seller activity is about the same cancelling each other out. A high earnings per share coupled with growth of earnings per share indicates a future filled with potential. As more buyers discover this bargain, buying will accelerate, driving the price up. Paying attention only to popularity an investor will never notice the value of the stock and will never muster the courage to buy it.

The second significate contradiction or divergence occurs when institutions are increasingly buying a stock and its price remains flat. When an investor finds a stock with high value, a flat price with institutional buying, consider it a real gem. The wise thing to do is to buy it.

It takes courage to continue to own a stock whose price is falling while it is gaining in value. Christopher H. Brown, in his book, *The Little Book of Value Investing*, cites a "study of 100,000 trades by the customers of Charles Schwab showed the stocks that customers sold were 3.4% higher one year later than the stocks they brought." This is a strong reminder not to give into fears and sell without considering value. It also takes courage to sell a stock whose price is rising while its value is falling below guidelines. Value is the starting point for decision making, not the current direction of stock prices.

Once I find a stock to buy. I use the VectorVest stock chart to find the last two dates when the stock fell significantly. I look up the earnings yield of the stock on those two dates. When stock approaches these earnings yields, I sell the stock. I keep track of the earnings yield of a stock on the following sample Earning Yield chart:

Stock	EY on Purchase date	Earnings yield on subsequent dates						
		1/19	1/26	2/2	2/9	2/16	2/23	3/1
ABC	17.12 – 1/12/2016	17.1	15.6	15.8	14.8	14.9	15.1	14.4

Notes:
On 10/2/15 EY was 8.1 when price peaked.
On 12/16/14 EY was 8.4 when price peaked.
I will sell when EY reaches 8.8.

I do an Earning Yield chart for every stock I own.

I have found moving averages to be useful. A moving average is determined by adding up the price of a stock each day and dividing it by the number of days, then plotting that average on a graph. (VectorVest allows a subscriber to design their individualized moving averages on their stock charts.) If the ten-day moving average moves up through a forty day moving average, I take this as an indication to buy. If a the daily price moves down through the ten day moving average, I take this as a possible indication to sell if the earnings yield has dropped off significantly.

VectorVest has developed a *Market Timing Index*, which is very helpful. The index measures timeliness on a scale of .1 to 2.0. The least timely is .1 and the timeliest is 2.0. I like to buy when the index has fallen below 1.0 and sell when the index is above 1.0. When the index reaches 1.5 it is time to start to accumulating cash and save up buying power for when the market bottoms out. The following chart below shows the results if you are lucky enough to buy when the index reaches its low and sell when it reaches its high.

Date	Market Timing Index	Buy or Sell	Stocks Ups/ Downs	Percent Gained	Investing $25,000
5/22/12	0.53	Buy			
9/18/12	1.55	Sell	9 Ups/ 1 Down	19.04%	$29,760
11/20/12	0.71	Buy			
1/22/13	1.57	Sell	10 Ups/ 0 Down	12.29%	$33,417
4/22/13	0.86	Buy			
5/22/13	1.46	Sell	8 Ups/ 2 Down	10.56%	$36,946
6/26/13	0.79	Buy			
7/26/13	1.51	Sell	8 Ups/ 2 Down	9.97%	$40,629
9/4/13	0.99	Buy			
9/20/13	1.51	Sell	7 Ups/ 3 Down	4.09%	$42,292

The portfolio grew 69.13% from 5/22/12 to 9/30/13 or at an annual rate of 55.23%. During this time period, all eight thousand stocks in the market grew an average of 26.36%. The Dow Jones Industrials grew 25.56%; the Russell 2000, 44.71%; and the S&P 500, 37.72%. The lesson to be earned is not trying to hit the highs and lows, but to try to time the buys while the market is down and the sells when the market is up. It is a trait that has to be acquired. It doesn't come naturally.

I also compare a stock's chart with the stock's industry chart. If the stock is doing better than the industry it is in, I consider that to be a plus. I avoid stock that has an irregular stock price pattern. Instead, I look for stocks with a steady long term price drift up or down. It is difficult to stay the course with a stock that experiences a lot of up and down prices occurring over a very short period of time. When the stock market is moving upward, it is much easier to show gains. If the stock market is moving downward, it becomes difficult to find stocks that will show a price gain.

A word of caution: reading stock charts can lead to a buying-selling obsession. Making money based on temporary prices requires the skill of a successful and experienced day trader. I have yet to find an amateur day trader who didn't eventually lose their shirt. (A day trader is someone who buys and sells the stock before the close of the same day.)

SHORT SELLERS

INSTITUTIONAL BUYERS AND sellers are one of the "elephants in the room"; they provide the demand to drive prices up and the selling pressure to drive prices down.

The other elephant in the room are short sellers. Short selling is defined as selling a stock one does not own. The short seller borrows the stock from another stockholder. The short seller must buy the stock back and return the stock to the owner by end of the next year. If the price of a stock is too high, short sellers are likely to step in and start selling the stock. Short selling can cause a panic, driving the price down further. Short sellers make their money when the stock price continues to fall after they sell the stock. Short sellers are smart and know what they are doing. Occasionally there is "good news" about a stock a short seller has sold. The stock price goes up instead of down. This is a short seller's nightmare because they will be forced to buy back the stock at a higher price.

If you think short sellers have made a mistake, you need to be extra careful before buying the stock. Short sellers are smart and it is very likely they know or see something you don't. It is always important to try to prove yourself wrong, rather than confirming you are right. For example, a few years ago I spotted a Russian telecom stock while reviewing shortsqueeze.com top 100 short sold stocks. (Shortsqueeze. com is a website that keeps track of short selling.) Seeing the telecom's stock prices going up instead of down, got me thinking, *this could be the situation where short sellers are wrong and their nightmare now exists. I can take advantage, buy the stock and make an excellent profit.* Shortsqueeze. com indicated 31.5% of this Russian stock's float was short. Float is all the stock a company has in the stock market being actively traded. It would take 26.5 days of average daily trading volume to buy this company's stock to cover the short sales. This represents a tremendous amount of pent-up buying power. However, short sellers are very good at what they do. Short sellers do occasionally make mistakes, but I had to be sure. I needed to start asking questions that would prove myself wrong.

Reviewing Yahoo Finance, I discovered the Russian telecom company's sales and profits had doubled in each of the last three years. During this time telecom stocks were in a great growth industry group. VectorVest gave the stock a relative value of 1.56. This was really great news. It appeared I was onto something really great. I was ready to buy.

Then I decided I had to follow the rule and try to prove myself wrong. The very first news article I found had the headline: "New York Stock Exchange May Force a Russian Telecom Stock to Delist." In 2002, in response to the Enron collapse, the Sarbanes-Oxley Act was passed. The act had detailed some very new and extensive disclosure requirements. The company claimed the costs of fulfilling the requirement of Sarbanes-Oxley too great and refused to fulfill the disclosure requirements. It is also very possible the stock had accounting problems that rivaled Enron's. If this stock was actually delisted on the New York Stock Exchange, the short sellers would be proved right. That is exactly what happened; the stock was delisted and the stock's price dropped.

"STUBBORN ASSUMPTIONS IMPED COMPREHENSION"

Alexander Hamilton

W E KNOW WHAT we are supposed to do, but we don't always do it. We have a tendency to make quick decisions and our emotions cause us to change course when our minds tell us not to do it. Instead of using newly learned information and methods, we fall back on old habits and assumptions. If we are to be successful, it is important we recognize what is going on, so we can overcome the ghosts that plague us.

Malcom Gladwell says the tendency is in our DNA which we inherited from our ancient ancestors. He makes the point our ancient ancestors' survived life and death situations by making very quick decisions. When a bear, lion or some other dangerous beast crossed their paths the choice was either to fight the beast or run to safety. It was our ancestors who ran and survived. The fighters perished. Today we still have the DNA causing us to make quick decisions. The problem as society gets more complex is there are so many factors to choose from we often chose the wrong factor to base our decision on. We need to learn the relevant information we should be using in our decision making. This requires re-learning what we have learned in the past and then practicing using the new techniques so they become natural to us.

Researchers says our brains are not fully developed until our mid or late twenties. Erica Hayasaki, a reporter for *Newsweek*, writes that the human brain is very plastic and absorbs a tremendous amount of knowledge in the first few years after child birth. And from age 15 to 30 there is another increase in plasticity making us able to consider new ideas, values and knowledge. After that our brains are pretty much fixed and wired. When we are young, we touch a hot stove burner—we hesitate for the rest of our lives to touch one again hot or cold. Our emotions take over our intellect.

We are wired to pay attention to our past experiences and many times it works against us when new information is presented. We fail because emotionally we can't seem to get past the biases we have accumulated over the years. Eventually, we have two choices: One throw up our hands and say, "I can't figure this out" and stop trying to invest in the stock market. The other is to say, "I am doing something wrong and I need to figure it out." If we chose the second option we first must ask questions. Are we being objective or are we using fear or hope in our decision making process? Are we paying attention to reality or are we being guided by our friends, co-workers and peers or what is being said in the newspapers or on TV and the radio? Are we willing to learn and put it into practice?

The World around us is complex. Rather than spending time to educate ourselves, we have learned to rely on street wisdom or what everyone else seems to know and accepted as true. It is accepted as fact with little or no research. I like going to the horse races. Horse bettors often say a horse coming off a mile in their last race into a shorter race the next time have a real advantage and win more often than not. Not knowing if this true, I kept track of horses coming off a mile for a whole racing season and discovered less than 5% of the time these horses actually win the next race. Bettors who know and pay attention to this information have an edge; they know 95% of the time, there is a better horse to bet on. If horse players place a wager on the horse coming off a mile and lose their bet, instead of blaming a bad ride on the jockey, they need to blame themselves for using known bad information.

It is paramount we use relevant evidence when making decisions— the evidence that works. Elizabeth Cobbs, author of the book *The Hamilton Affair,* said it best when explaining the concepts Alexander Hamilton tried to live by, "…Prejudice and ignorance are the brick and mortar of men's prisons." And "…stubborn assumptions imped comprehension." We do have to be willing to give up long held beliefs and be open to learning something new. For many that is very hard to do because who we are, the assumptions we make has grown out of our past environment and what we perceive our self-interests to be: whether we live in a big city or in rural area; whether we attend church or not; whether we are a union member, or a small business person, or work for a large company in mid-management; whether we watch Fox news, or MSNBC, or CNN; whether we teach school, or are a policeman, or a fireman, or work in the private sector; whether we are in good health or poor health; whether we are a man or a woman; whether we earn minimum wages or have a million dollar salary or somewhere in between; whether we went to college or not. If we are willing to learn we have to put many of these influences and experiences aside and consider other viewpoints. Only then can we find the evidence that really matters and be comfortable using it.

STOCK MARKET AND PRESIDENTIAL TERMS

J OHN WOODEN, THE famous UCLA coach said, "The best are willing to learn after they have learned." With all the new ways to communicate, the logical conclusion would be, it is easier to see the World as it is, but that is not the way it is. We tend to only pay attention to news that supports our political, religious or cultural beliefs. Doing this makes the world clearer, simpler and easy to understand. There is a sign in one of my favorite restaurants: "Warning—an open mind may cause your brains to fall out." It is humorous as it describes our thirst for clarity and meaning. It is also a statement about our resistance to understanding why others have viewpoints that are different from ours.

Editors and publishers are in the business to make a profit. The only way to sell advertising is to have other businesses willing to advertise to their audience. The best way to have a lot of listeners and readers is to give people news that supports their way of thinking or believing. Today so much of our news is more than just slanted—it has become advocacy oriented. "News" organizations have discovered that big money can be made if emotions and beliefs can be exploited. The goal is to have their audiences to become addicted to their programming. There is no better way to control thinking or emotions than to play on what makes you happy, sad or mad. Emotions become the narcotic that creates the addiction. Evidence, reality take a backseat. It becomes difficult to see the World as it is, causing our perception of current events to fall short of reality.

An investor who has learned to have an open mind does have an advantage. It is a skill that can be acquired. Ken Fisher, billionaire investment manager and author of the book *The Only Three Questions That Count,* says that investors should be reading the news with an eye to prove themselves wrong.

It is hard to judge whether or not the business climate is improving or declining. At any given time, there are some who say we are in a decline, while others say things are improving. Presidential terms are four years long and have a clear beginning and ending. A close examination of the presidential election cycle leads to some very surprising and predictable conclusions. Rasmussen Reports polls show Republicans have a four percentage point advantage among investors while Democrats have eighteen point advantage among non-investors. Since investors tend to be Republicans, can one infer Republicans are better for investors?

When I redid a single chart prepared from information gathered from Global Financial Data by Ken Fisher, splitting them into two charts listing the presidents by political party since the formation of the S&P 500, some very interesting information emerged.

The Effect of Republican Presidential Terms on the Stock Market

President	First Year	Second Year	Third Year	Fourth Year	Overall
Hoover	1929 -8.4%	1930 -24.9%	1931 -43.3%	1932 -8.2%	-21.2%
Eisenhower	1953 -1.0%	1954 +54.6%	1955 +31.6%	1956 +6.6%	+23.0%
Eisenhower	1957 -10.8%	1958 +43.4%	1959 +12.0%	1960 +0.5%	+11.3%
Nixon	1969 -8.5%	1970 +4.0%	1971 +14.3%	1972 +19.0%	+ 7.2%
Nixon-Ford	1973 -14.7%	1974 -26.5%	1975 +37.2%	1976 +23.8%	+ 5.0%
Reagan	1981 - 4.9%	1982 +21.4%	1983 +22.5%	1984 +23.4%	+15.6%
Reagan	1985 +32.2%	1986 +18.5%	1987 + 5.2%	1988 +16.8%	+18.2%
First Bush	1989 +31.5%	1990 - 3.2%	1991 +30.6%	1992 + 7.6%	+16.6%
Second Bush	2001 -11.9%	2002 -22.1%	2003 +28.7%	2004 +10.9%	+ 5.6%
Second Bush	2005 + 4.9%	2006 +12.0%	2007 + 0.9%	2008 -42.2%	- 6.1%
Average	+ 0.9%	+ 7.8%	+14.0%	+ 5.39%	+ 7.2%
Number Up Years	3	6	9	8	26
Number Down Years	7	4	1	2	14

There have been forty years of Republican presidents since the S&P 500 index came into being. Investing ten thousand dollars and compounding the interest of 7.2% during these Republican years would have turn the $10,000 into $161,358. Investing $100 a month during the forty years would have returned $261,997. The results are not that bad! You can't stop here and be satisfied. You have to ask the question, "What about the stock market during the forty years of Democratic presidential rule?"

The Effect of Democratic Presidential Terms on the Stock Market

The Democrats	First Year	Second Year	Third Year	Fourth Year	Overall
FDR	1933 +54.0%	1934 - 1.5%	1935 +47.7%	1936 +33.9%	+33.5%
FDR	1937 -35.0%	1938 +31.1%	1939 - 0.4%	1940 - 9.8%	- 3.5%
FDR	1941 -11.6%	1942 +20.3%	1943 +25.9%	1944 +19.8%	+13.6%
FDR-Truman	1945 +36.4%	1946 - 8.1%	1947 + 5.7%	1948 + 5.5%	+ 9.9%
Truman	1949 +18.8%	1950 +31.7%	1951 +24.0%	1952 +18.4%	+ 9.9%
Kennedy-Johnson	1961 +26.6%	1962 - 8.7%	1963 +22.8%	1964 +16.6%	+14.4%
Johnson	1965 +12.5%	1966 - 10.1%	1967 +24.0%	1968 +11.1%	+ 9.4%
Carter	1977 - 7.2%	1966 + 6.6%	1979 +18.4%	1980 +32.4%	+12.6%
Clinton	1993 +10.0%	1994 + 1.3%	1995 +37.5%	1996 +22.9%	+17.9%
Clinton	1997 +33.3%	1998 +28.6%	1999 +21.0%	2000 - 9.1%	+18.5%
Obama	2009 +29.5%	2010 +18.3%	2011 - 2.35%	2012 +14.9%	+15.1%
Average	+15.2	+10.0%	+20.4%	+14.3%	+15.0%
Up Years	8	7	9	9	33
Down Years	3	4	2	2	11

Under the Republicans, investments doubled every ten years or doubled four times during their forty years. Under Democrats, investments doubled eight and half times. Ten thousand dollars invested during the forty Democratic years turned in $2,304,667. This is an incredible two million dollars or 8.7 times more than the Republican forty years. Adding on the Obama years brings the balance to $4,037,345. Investing a $100 a month though-out the forty years brings a balance of $2,678,635. Adding on the Obama years raises the total to $4,684,950.

Ignoring the fact many business leaders are said to be Democrats, i.e., Warren Buffett, Costco's Jim Sinegal or Zumiez's Tom Compion; when I show the two charts to Republicans and Democrats both seem very surprised. This is not what has been told over and over. Republicans in particular say these charts make no sense. They point out everyone knows Republican policies support free enterprise while Democrats are about regulations, taxes on the rich and social welfare programs.

We need to ask are the charts an aberration or is there more evidence that support this result. Finding out the answer requires an examination of the assumptions we often make about free markets and government activity. The business cycle is driven more by businesses either overdoing or underdoing business activity rather than government policy (for example having too little or too much inventory, incurring too little or too much debt or extending too little or too much credit). For example, we focus on too much government debt burdening our future children and driving the forces of inflation. We seldom pay attention to the size of private debt. Free markets depend upon the ability to incur debt. There are times when private debt grows so large the private sector cannot pay off the debt. This can lead to disastrous times. Both the great depression starting in 1929 and the great recession of 2008 were not the result of the collapse of public debt or government failure. Both were the result of the collapse of private debt. In 1929 railroads began to fail to pay their bonded debt payments. Banks started to fail in large numbers because of this; credit was no longer available; private debt fell 44.3% between 1929 and 1932. Farms and businesses were forced to sell their products at cascading lower prices. As a result, many suffered bankrupting losses. By 1933, tax revenue fell 48.3%, government expenses were 131% greater than taxes. Between 1929 and 1933, GNP fell 47.3%, personal consumption fell 40.3% and unemployment rose to 25%.

In 2008, private debt equaled 350% of GNP, and again problems not from public debt. It was the private home mortgage market that collapsed. Again the United States was faced with possibility of private debt shrinking 40%. Fortunately, both Presidents Bush and Obama paid attention to the experience of the great depression and were unafraid to use public debt to prop up the private sector. Knowing this history and acting accordingly gives the economy a leg up. Investors paying attention can take advantage of the situation. Allowing your decision to be dictated by political purity can be very dangerous to your ability to make the right decisions in the stock market.

To get back to the question: Is there any other evidence life may be better under Democrats? The chart below shows Gross National Product growth under Republican and Democratic presidents.

Effect of Presidential Fiscal Policies On Percent Growth of GNP since WW II

President	First Year	Second Year	Third Year	Fourth Year	Average
Repubicans					
Eisenhower 1st Term	0.3%	8.9%	5.5%	5.0%	5.1%
Eisenhower 2nd Term	1.3%	8.4%	3.9%	3.4%	4.3%
Nixon	5.4%	8.4%	9.8%	11.7%	8.8%
Nixon/Ford	8.4%	9.2%	11.4%	11.3%	10.1%
Reagan 1st Term	4.1%	8.9%	11.2%	11.3%	7.8%
Reagan 2nd Term	5.8%	6.2%	7.6%	7.4%	6.8%
1st Bush	6.3%	4.6%	5.7%	6.3%	5.3%
2nd Bush 1st Term	3.5%	4.7%	6.5%	6.5%	5.3%
2nd Bush 2nd Term	5.1%	2.6%	-2.3%	2.7%	2.0%
Totals	4.5%	6.8%	6.6%	6.8%	6.2%
Democrats					
Truman 2nd Term	9.7%	15.7%	5.6%	5.8%	9.2%
Kennedy/Johnson	7.5%	5.4%	7.4%	8.4%	7.2%
Johnson	5.4%	8.4%	9.8%	11.4%	8.8%
Carter	12.7%	11.7%	8.8%	12.1%	11.3%
Clinton 1st Term	6.3%	4.6%	5.7%	6.3%	5.7%
Clinton 2nd Term	5.5%	8.6%	6.4%	3.4%	6.0%
Totals	7.8%	9.1%	7.3%	8.0%	8.0%

Source: United States Bureau of Economic Analysis

A study of after-tax incomes using constant dollars (taking out the effect of inflation) since 1941 by Larry Bartels of the Wilson School of Public Affairs, gives an interesting insight to this question. If you are in a family with an income in the lower 20% of families, on average your yearly income grew 0.6% under Republican presidents and 2.63% under Democratic presidents. If you are in a family whose income is in the top 5% of families, your yearly income grew 2.05% under Republican presidents and 2.63% under Democratic presidents. If you are in a family whose income is between the bottom 20% and top 5%, your yearly income grew 1.28% under Republicans and 2.41% under Democrats.

Effect of Presidential Fiscal Policies On Net Job Creation since WW II

President	First Year	Second Year	Third Year	Fourth Year	Average
Republicans					
Eisenhower (1st Term)	2.9%	-2.4%	3.4%	3.4%	1.8%
Eisenhower (2nd Term)	0.9%	-2.9%	3.8%	1.7%	0.9%
Nixon	3.7%	0.7%	0.5%	3.5%	2.1%
Nixon/Ford	4.2%	1.9%	-1.7%	3.2%	1.9%
Reagan 1st Term	0.8%	-1.8%	0.7%	4.7%	1.1%
Reagan 2nd Term	3.2%	2.0%	2.6%	3.2%	2.8%
1st Bush	2.5%	1.4%	-1.0%	0.3%	0.8%
2nd Bush	0.0%	-1.1%	-0.3%	-0.6%	-0.5%
Totals	2.3%	-0.3%	1.0%	2.4%	1.4%
Democrats					
Roosevelt/Truman	-3.6%	3.1%	5.2%	2.3%	1.8%
Truman	-2.5%	3.3%	5.8%	2.0%	2.2%
Kennedy/Johnson	-0.4%	2.9%	2.0%	2.9%	1.9%
Johnson	4.3%	5.2%	3.0%	3.2%	3.9%
Carter	3.9%	5.1%	3.6%	0.7%	3.3%
Clinton 1st Term	1.9%	3.1%	2.6%	2.4%	2.5%
Clinton 2nd Term	2.6%	2.6%	2.4%	2.2%	2.5%
Averages	0.9%	3.6%	3.5%	2.2%	2.6%

Source: US Bureau of Statistics

There are two distinct reactions when I show these charts to people. One reaction is pain; they quickly dismiss the information as political hogwash. The other reaction is to study the charts at length.

In general, Democrats support demand-side economic policies. Meaning they believe the economy grows from the bottom up. It is consumer buying power that drives economic prosperity. The democratic instincts are to protect the consumer, promote better wages and to keep the buying public healthy.

Republicans believe the economy grows from the top down or supply side economics; that prosperity trickles and jobs trickle down from profits. It is a "you build it and they will come" philosophy. It is producers' profits that drives hiring. The Republican instincts are to be wary of consumerism and government policy.

Problems do arise when each begin to not hear what the other has to say. It is our ability to compromise that makes us strong. It is a mistake to blame financial shortcomings both when investing in the stock market or in your private business on the political party in power. No one should pull out of the market just because a Democrat or Republican is elected. Doing so is paying attention to your emotions driven by political commentary; not to financial information of individual companies. Compare the High Quality back-test with the performance of the S&P 500.

Year	President	S&P 500	High Quality Stocks	High Quality Stock under $25
2000	Clinton	- 9.1%	26.4%	52.2%
2001	W. Bush	-11.9%	55.5%	65.1%
2002	W. Bush	-22.1%	8.0%	12.1%
2003	W. Bush	28.1%	120.6%	136.7%
2004	W. Bush	10.9%	46.8%	47.7%
2005	W. Bush	4.9%	39.6%	46.5%
2006	W. Bush	12.0%	24.6%	49.2%
2007	W. Bush	0.9%	5.5%	11.9%
2008	W. Bush	-42.2%	-45.5%	-48.5%
2009	Obama	29.5%	75.8%	88.6%

DONALD L. HINMAN

Whether you succeed in business or the stock market is based on the ability to pay attention to the evidence that points to reality and taking control. The third and fourth years of a presidential term produce the best results. During the first two years of a Democratic president the stock market does much better than that of the Republican presidents. There is no doubt free market economies outperform any other system. There is also no doubt high performing free markets depend upon a sensible system of governing.

HISTORICAL FISCAL POLICY LESSONS

THE PREVIOUS CHAPTER shows statistics government taxing and spending policies have on the economy and the stock market. It is not about who is right or wrong. It is about understanding the many sides of the argument. And the willingness to see the other's viewpoint in the debate. The strength of our economy comes from having a diversity of opinions and being able to find compromises. When we believe our side is the only way and we fail to find compromises is when the problems start to accumulate.

An investor needs to gain an understanding of fiscal policy or the effect taxing and spending policies have on the economy. Cable news gives us more alternatives to discover what is going on. Unfortunately, what is said is what audiences want to hear, not on what they need to hear. It is human nature to want to hear that which supports how you think things are. Too often we see only one side of the argument instead of being well rounded in our understanding of the World, we have a less understanding of the World than we should have.

What is passed off as being lessons in economics, is not economists speaking at all. This causes considerable confusion about whether or not economics is a science. Being an economics major, I can say there is solid agreement among economists (whether they are considered conservative or liberal) about effect of fiscal policies. The effect of raising taxes and cutting government spending is the same—it dampens growth. The effect of cutting taxes and increasing spending is the same—it stimulates growth. The difference comes in deciding whose taxes are cut or raised or what programs are cut or increased. Mark Zandi, Moody's chief economist and John McCain's economic advisor, points out each fiscal policy option has its own effect. Spending a $100 extending unemployment causes the economy to grow $173; a $100 of infrastructure spending creates a $159 of economic growth; a $100 tax cut for the wealthy grows the economy an additional $31; and sending a $100 aid to state and local governments produces $173 of economic growth.

Democrats believe in the power of demand-side forces in our economy. So when hard times hit Democratic leaders stress the importance of extending unemployment, increasing infrastructure spending and aid to state and local governments. The thinking behind their policies is economic growth is powered by increased consumer buying. Strong wages and salaries lead to strong sales. Democrats also want labor to share in the benefits of increased productivity. They believe using productivity to strengthen wages will lead to more sales and strengthening profits.

History shows purchasing power is the key to a stronger and quicker recovery. The Great Depression demonstrated the worthiness of using demand-side economics to stem a business decline. President Hoover, a businessman-engineer, in first three years in office insisted on a balance budget, believing it would turn the economy around. If President Hoover had been running a corporation, his strategy would have worked and would have been a sensible path to increased profits. This gives the company an opportunity to expand and hire more people in the future. The laid off employees can recover by seeking employment elsewhere.

He was not running a company; he was running an economy. In an economy cutting government spending below tax revenues leads to jobs being lost with no place for laid off workers to find a job as every employer is laying off workers. Fewer workers means less consumer buying power. Less consumer buying means falling business sales. The end result is the whole economy shrinks. That is precisely what happened during the Hoover years. The stock market fell 8.4% in 1929; fell 24.9% in 1930; fell 41.3% in 1931; and fell 8.2% in 1932. President Hoover relented and let spending exceed taxes by 142% in 1932 and by 131% in 1933; enabling the stock market to rise 54% in 1933.

In 1936 under President Roosevelt, federal government spending doubled tax revenues. The number of people employed grew 14.7% the next two years. The stock market grew 48% in 1935 and 34% in 1936.

A coalition of Republicans and conservative southern Democrats took control of Congress in 1937. This coalition forced the federal budget to be balanced. In 1938, the budget expenditures exceeded revenue by 1.3%. The number of people employed dropped 5.9% in 1938. The stock market fell 37.1% in 1938.

Republicans, business owners, managers and many editorial writers identify with supply-side economics. Supply siders push for taxing cuts, particularly for the wealthy. The idea is the wealthy will use the money to build new things. The supply side theme is literally the *Field of Dreams* approach, "build it and they will come." As Mark Zandi points out cutting the wealthy's taxes only produces an additional thirty cents for every dollar cut. This explains the reality, if tax cuts are given with no incentives the wealthy often invest in something other than job creating assets. Tax cuts for wealthy are about new wealth creation, not jobs creation.

Supply-side thinkers discount the importance of expanding labor's purchasing power as a source for creating new sales and expanding the economy. Instead, they worry the effect increased labor costs will have on business expenses. They point out lower expenses lead to greater profits. Businesses with strong profits can expand, but it is not a guaranteed outcome. Profits alone are not an incentive to expand or increase payroll. In my years of business experience, I like other businessmen are unwilling invest in new employees unless there is a certainty, it will lead to more returns or profits.

Demand-siders believe the key to a strong economy is increasing purchasing power at the bottom. There is a strong argument that building wealth at the top siphons off purchasing power at bottom. China's recent success is rooted in recognizing this. They have used their newly earned wealth to buy U.S. Treasury bonds. This puts money back into the American economy. This has the effect of increasing the purchasing power of the American consumer.

Raising taxes on the wealthy does not have the predicted effect of shrinking the economy many supply-siders stress will happen. President Bill Clinton urged and a Democratic Congress agreed and passed a higher income tax for wealthy Americans. The result was during the eight Clinton years, 22.7 million new jobs were created and the stock market was up an average of 18.7% a year. President George W. Bush early in his administration pushed for a tax cut with a disproportionate share going to wealthy Americans. During the eight years of George W. Bush, new job creation fell from 22.7 million created during the Clinton years to 1.1 million. The stock market dropped to a negative 0.25% per year average.

Deficit spending can lead to inflation if the money supply grows faster than the ability of the economy to produce goods and services. Free trade adds to the availability of goods and services, exerting downward pressure on prices and services and has a positive effect of controlling inflation in spite of constant deficit spending by the federal government. Free trade also has the effect of keeping middle class wages lower while improving profits of international companies. The American worker has been put into direct competition with lower, third world wages. The spread between American's high incomes and low incomes is widening to record levels. When President Clinton's increased taxes on the wealthy, it caused job creation and a healthy stock market. It can be argued raising taxes gave an incentive to the wealthy to avoid paying taxes by investing in American depreciation-able assets thereby, causing more American jobs and more sales for American companies. While raising taxes is argued to be an incentive for businesses to invest in job creating assets, it is also counter-intuitive.

During President George W. Bush's two terms, there was a lack of understanding about the importance of creating purchasing power through government policy. Many of the books I have read about the Iraqi war reconstruction and reconstruction of New Orleans after the hurricane damage, the authors emphasized that the insurgency took hold in Iraq after the invasion because local Iraqis became incensed that foreign labor was being used to build Iraq instead of local labor. This drove the unemployment rate in Iraq to as high as 80%, the atmosphere became a breeding ground for insurgent recruiting.

The revitalization of New Orleans was slower than expected because the government awarded reconstruction contracts to contractors who imported workers from areas outside of New Orleans. The labor dollars did not stay in the New Orleans area to stimulate its economy.

President Obama, immediately upon coming into office, talked Congress into passing a stimulus spending bill. The effect on the economy and stock market was markedly different from the Reagan tax cut in his first year in office. The S&P 500 fell 4.9% compared to 2009 when the S&P 500 rose 35.8%. Many small investors who did not support President Obama were not convinced. Two years into the Obama administration Yahoo Finance reported while large investors resumed their investing, small investors were very reluctant stock market investors. In April, 2010 contributions to mutual funds were still down 5%. Small investors who allowed their politics to affect their investing decisions missed out on an opportunity for real profits. Fourteen months into the Obama administration, the S&P 500 was up 40%. My stock portfolio was up 140%. The information about the first year of a Democratic president only reinforced my investment inclinations. I was handsomely rewarded for paying attention to this evidence.

We tend to blame our failures and give credit for successes on whether or not our favorite political party holds power. In reality whether we experience success or failure is more likely the result of our person, business and investing decisions.

THE EFFECT OF REGULATIONS

THERE IS ALWAYS a lot of talk about how regulations hold us back. It is easy to get a businessman to agree government regulations discourage the profit incentive. Those who support deregulation assert their belief the invisible hand of the market will even out any inequities. Running my insurance agency, I am often frustrated with insurance regulations. I do have to admit, regulations also make my business life more coherent and orderly. It is the "rules of the game" that assure fair competition. I cannot imagine what a basketball or football game would be like with no rules.

Recent history shows that an economy with few or no regulations gives an edge and rewards corner-cutting, unethical and even criminal behavior. Alice Schroeder writes in the book *The Snowball* that Warren Buffett in 1967 listened to a speech Dr. Martin Luther King gave at Grinnell College in Iowa. Dr. King stated, "The laws are not to change the heart but to restrain the heartless." From that point forward, Warren Buffett used this thought as his theme. Honesty of management became paramount in his consideration of whether or not to invest in a company.

In FDR's first term, the government began regulating the stock market, making sure companies are open and honest about their operations. Only two times in seventy-two years has the market been down more than two years in a row. Each time the downturn lasted three years. Eliminate these six years and the market was up 80% of the time. Otherwise it has been up 70% of the time. Our investment strategy should be designed to take advantage of the up years. How long does an "up market" stay up? Shouldn't we, on general principle, get defensive after four or five years—maybe a shorter period of, like, three years?

If you flip a coin and heads come up nine times in a row, many gamblers will bet on the tenth flip as if the odds are nine to one, tails will come up. Actually, the odds remain two to one. I learned this the hard way when I first got married. With her usual luck, my wife was up at the roulette table. She had me hold her nice size pot of money while she went to powder her nose. Roulette wheels have a bet on either black or red numbers. While she was gone, I saw the roulette ball stop on red six times in a row. I thought opportunity is knocking, I can double my wife's money and give her a nice surprise if I put all her winnings on black, thinking there is no way the ball can stop on red seven times in a row. But it did. My wife's surprise was something other than nice. No longer am I ever trusted with my wife's winnings at a casino. (Actually, she does not let me handle the family's checkbook.)

Getting defensive based solely upon the number of years the market is up is very risky business. You could miss out on a lot of good years.

President or Presidents	Length of time the market is up
1st Bush and Clinton	9 years
Reagan and 1st Bush	8 years
FDR and Truman	6 years
Truman	5 years
FDR	4 years
Eisenhower	4 years
Kennedy and Johnson	3 years
Nixon	3 years
Carter	3 years
Nixon and Ford	2 years

Many of the stock market regulations did not exist prior to the stock market crash in 1929. In the 1930's, the Security Exchange Commission developed many rules focused on making sure public companies were open in their dealings.

Republicans gained control of Congress in the 1990's and began a push for deregulation. In the waning days of the Clinton administration, the banking industry embraced Republican Senator Phil Gramm's budget bill amendment deregulating credit swaps. Credit swaps insure loans, protecting the lenders from borrowers who are unable to make loan payments. Business writer David Corn says this generated a sixty-two billion dollar exposure for insurance companies. This was four times the size of the entire stock market. With the swap deregulation, no one knew if the insurance companies that sold swaps had the money to pay claims.

Banks began to loosen their loan requirements, believing their loans insured by swaps would be protected from a borrower unable to make their payments. It turned out credit swap insurers did not have nearly enough money to cover the bad loans. Suddenly, the banking system ran out of money. Credit became frozen, triggering the stock market collapse of 2008 in a magnitude not seen since 1929.

President George W. Bush knowing the mistakes made in 1929 by President Hoover, went against his party's instincts and pushed through a $700 billion bailout of the finance industry. President Obama used some of the bailout to save both General Motors and Chrysler. The bailout used a combination of loans and buying preferred stock. Originally the final cost to the taxpayer was estimated to be $500 billion dollars. In the end, the government actually made a profit.

There is considerable historical precedent for the government to buy preferred stock, and as times get better, the company issues and sells common stock to buy back the preferred stock or, the government sells the preferred stock to investors. The United States did this in the 1930's to save and stabilize banks. Both European and Asian countries did it in the 1990's to save banks and vital industries. Japan used a variation of this in 2002 when the central bank of Japan literally printed money to buy mortgages, treasury bonds, and bonds of companies to ease or reduce the quantity of assets. The effect drove asset prices up and jump-started the Japanese economy.

Some argue this is an improper use of the government saying businesses should have the right to fail. And if they do fail, bankruptcy is the punishment for taking chances. A question could also be asked: Should businesses and individuals be forced into bankruptcy when it is not the result of their failings, but because of someone else's unknowable and uncontrollable poor decision making? It is easy to jump to the conclusion that regulations are unnecessary and harmful to the interaction of the market. The truth of the matter is the government is the only protection the small stock market investor may have. As small investors, we don't have the power of the institutional investor to punish management or affect company policies. We depend upon government regulations to make sure financial reporting of a company is accurate, transparent and fraudulent behavior is punished.

UNDERSTANDING MONETARY POLICY

F EW PEOPLE KNOW about or pay attention to monetary policy. When most think of money issues, they relate their discussion to cash flow problems they encounter in their family budgets and businesses. People do pay attention to interest rates. As interest rates fall they refinance their homes, buy more expensive homes and are more likely to make major purchases. Most, however, have little knowledge as to what are the forces that drive interest rates up or down. In my business, our cash flow is directly connected to our ability to stay in business. When cash flow margins narrow, I worry. Anyone who runs a business or household know without sufficient cash flow to pay bills, it is a road to bankruptcy. We usually think our ability to obtain a loan is connected to whether or not we have sufficient income to pay the loan off. There is more to it. It is also connected to the ability of the banking system to make the loan. In the past there have been many times when banks did not have the resources to make loans. It had little to do with the credit worthiness of the person or company applying for the loan.

National governments can operate much differently than individuals or private businesses. Most national governments are sovereigns. They have the power to create and regulate the money supply. Section 8 of the United States Constitution gives Congress the sovereign power "to coin money, regulate the value thereof." This function of government is called monetary policy. Congress has passed this power on to the Federal Reserve. The Federal Reserve (Fed) is a central bank. Congress's charge to the Fed is maintaining sound monetary conditions so the economy will be stable and have a better chance to be prosperous. The Fed's policy should be based upon sound business and economic policies. Their decisions need to be made in an atmosphere totally free from political pressures.

There is always a drumbeat for a return to a currency backed by gold or silver. Arguing in the "good old gold standard days" before the

Fed Reserve, there were no economic ups and downs; it was a time of common decency, simple relationships and fiscal responsibility. History shows something much different.

The National Bureau of Economic Research reports, from 1854 to 1914 there were fifteen recessions lasting an average of twenty-two months with an average recovery of little over twenty-four months. Money and banking were unregulated—resulting in runaway boom times, followed by collapses, bank panics and runs on banks. Many families lost their hard-earned deposits during the bank runs while loan foreclosures continued. Robber barons dominated—unfairly building monopolies and massive fortunes. President Teddy Roosevelt was talking about robber barons when he said, "Walk softly and carry a big stick."

In 1913 the Federal Reserve was created. From 1915 to 1933 there were five recessions lasting an average of eighteen months.

In 1933 the FDIC began insuring deposits. From 1934 to 2010 there were twelve recessions lasting an average of ten months.

Monetary policy has evolved since the Federal Reserve was formed. From the end of World War II to the Carter administration the main goal of the Fed was maintaining full employment. President Carter inherited a serious inflation problem from previous administrations when he took office. During his administration, Congress adjusted full employment goals by adding a co-goal of controlling inflation. As this goal was implemented, interest rates skyrocketed causing considerable pain among the business community. President Carter was blamed for most of the painful business downturn. Since inflation was brought under control, we have enjoyed a long period of no inflation. President Carter also began the process of removing trade barriers. The result has been a long period of little or no inflation. I have always felt President Carter deserves to be recognized for his courage taking the steps to turn around a very bad situation. Over time history will probably shine a much better light on the Carter administration.

The Federal Reserve's control of the money supply is accomplished largely through the control of member bank reserves. Member banks are the banks we find in every town across America. Member banks are required to hold a certain percentage of total checking account deposits in cash or in a reserve account with the Federal Reserve. The Fed can raise the member banks the reserve account up or down. For example if there is a 14% reserve requirement; and if a bank has a total of $100,000 in customers' checking accounts, it must have $14,000 cash on hand or in a reserve account with the Fed.

Using the same example, a bank has $14,000 cash and $50,000 deposits in their customers' checking accounts; can make $50,000 in new loans. If a customer came into the bank and made a $10,000 loan. The bank would make the loan by making the following accounting entries: increase "Loans to Customers" by $10,000 and increase "Customers' Deposits" by $10,000. Note that no money was ever taken out of cash and given to the customer. The bank did increase the overall money supply in the economy by $10,000. This does seem like black magic. The banking system works because banks only make loans they are certain will be paid bank. Banking regulations make sure this happens. Without financial integrity the whole banking system would fall apart. In the 1980's, Savings and Loan banks were deregulated. Within a few years, bank fraud became pervasive causing many Savings and Loan banks to fail.

Our money system is not tied to gold or silver. A dynamic economy requires a dynamic money supply. A growing economy requires a growing money supply. If demand for goods and services grows too fast and production of the goods and services cannot keep up this will cause inflation. The Fed regulating the supply of money becomes the regulator of economic growth. The Fed has many tools to regulate growth or the lack of growth.

The Fed may rise or lower the reserve requirement of member banks. Lowering the reserve requirement gives the banks an ability to make more loans. Raising the reserve requirement restricts the ability of banks to make loans. It is the ability to create or shrink bank reserves that is the distinguishing feature of a central bank.

Another tool of the Fed is open market operations. It buys or sells United States government securities. Buying U.S. government securities gives member banks more reserves to make more loans. Selling U.S. government securities lowers member banks reserves.

If a member bank finds itself short of the required cash. The member bank may borrow from other banks or the Fed to cover the shortage. The interest charged to the member bank is called the re-discount rate. Raising the re-discount rate has a slow-down effect on the economy. Lowering the re-discount rate has the effect of speeding-up the economy.

The Fed may also put "selective controls" by requiring a loan made by a bank to be used for a specific purpose. The weakness of this tool is it limits the free choice of the bank customer. The Fed may use moral suasion or influence by requesting member banks to tighten up their reserves voluntarily.

The history of the Federal Reserve has proven America has the ability to blend the ingenuity of the private market with the safety of regulations protecting the common good. This ability is responsible for producing the world's greatest economy with the highest standard of living.

Until the middle of President Carter's term, the stated goal of the Fed was full employment. If unemployment grew the Fed would increase the money supply. If we had full employment money supply growth would be restricted.

Prior to President Carter taking office inflation had been gathering steam. During his term inflation was approaching runaway proportions, as a result controlling inflation was added as a dual goal of the Fed. Interest rates rose to historical highs. At the same time, President Carter deregulated many industries and opened up free trade. The effect on the stock market was favorable. The third and fourth years of his term the S&P 500 grew 18.4% and 32.4% respectively. The 32.4% actually beat President Reagan's best year 32.2%. When I remind people of this, it is met with disbelief.

Conventional wisdom is that a drop in interest rates will cause stocks to go up. And a rise in interest rates will cause the stock market to drop. All that changed when the Federal Reserve begin to guard against inflation. To demonstrate, the following two charts show the annual changes in the federal fund rates and its effect on the S&P 500 from 1956 to 2006.

The Effect of the Federal Reserve Policy to Change Interest Rates to Maintain Full Employment on the Stock Market (1956 – 1978)

Years Interest Rates Went Up		Years Interest Rate Went Down	
Years	S&P Growth	Years	S&P Growth
1956	6.6%	1958	43.4%
1957	-10.8%	1961	26.9%
1959	12.0%	1967	24.0%
1960	+.5%	1970	4.0%
1962	- 8.7%	1971	14.3%
1963	22.8%	1972	19.0%
1965	12.5%	1975	37.2%
1966	-10.1%	1976	23.8%
1968	11.1%		
1969	- 8.5%		
1973	-14.7%		
1974	-26.5%		
1977	- 7.2%		
1978	6.6%		
Average	0.1%		24.1%

The stock market from 1956 through 1978 grew an average of 10.2% each year. There was solid evidence that lowering interest rates produced a positive effect the stock market. Rising interest rates caused the stock market to perform in a sub-par fashion. Did this trend continue when the Fed began guarding against inflation?

The effect of the Federal Reserve Policy to Change Interest Rates to Maintain Full Employment and Control Inflation on the Stock Market (1979-2005)

Years Interest Rates Go Up		Years Interest Rates Go Down	
Year	S&P 500 Growth	Year	S&P 500 Growth
1979	18.4%	1982	21.4%
1980	32.4%	1983	22.5%
1981	-4.9%	1985	32.2%
1984	23.4%	1986	18.5%
1988	16.8%	1987	5.2%
1989	31.5%	1990	-3.2%
1994	1.3%	1991	30.6%
1995	37.5%	1992	7.6%
1997	33.3%	1993	10.0%
2000	-9.1%	1996	22.9%
2004	10.9%	1998	28.6%
2005	4.5%	1999	21.0%
2001	-11.9%		
2002	-22.1%	2003	28.9%
Average	16.3%		14.1%

The changing of Federal Reserve goals, deregulation of businesses and opening up free trade has had a dramatic effect on the market's response to interest rate changes. The average annual growth of the stock market has risen from 10.2% before 1979 to 15.1% after. Since 1979, the stock market has actually done slightly better when interest rates rise. The market seems to respond favorably if it agrees with Fed action.

THE EFFECT OF TRADE POLICIES

D URING THE REAGAN administration the United States switched from being a creditor nation to being a debtor nation. This made foreign manufactured products more attractive. This was good for the American consumer. This was bad for the American worker. Being in competition with third World employees dampened wage increases for American workers while creating opportunities for international companies to make more profits. The country's trade balance shifted from a surplus to a deficit. It also solved the inflation problem that had been plaguing our economy for several decades. Every year since more of the products we consume in the United States are produced overseas. To buy more goods produced overseas and sell less goods overseas takes money. As American public debt grows, foreign countries still find U.S. treasury bonds to be safe and profitable. China and Japan are the biggest holders of our public debt.

One of the main reasons, beyond believing it is a safe haven for their money, is they buy American public debt to give Americans the money to buy their products. This raises the purchasing power of the dollar, lowering the value of the yuan and yen, making Chinese and Japanese products less expensive in the United States and our products more expensive worldwide. Large United States corporations have profited from lower labor costs. At the same time it has worked against the American worker as they have found themselves in competition with foreign workers. The gap between the American wealthy and not so American wealthy grows to be more every year. One way for the American worker to fight back is to invest in the stock market sharing in the large corporation's profits. *This is why this book is so important.*

If America's families' income will not cover their purchases, they either have to sell something, use credit cards or remortgage their homes to keep up. For years homeowners did just that, they refinanced their homes. Unlike the government which can print money, homeowners have use their earnings to pay off their credit card debt and home mortgages. In 2008, the American consumer became tapped out. Many could not make their mortgage and credit card payments. A debt crisis ensued. The stock market suffered losses not seen since the days of President Hoover in the late 1920's.

One important defense against a trade imbalance has been to let the value of the dollar float. Let the market determine the value of the dollar against other currencies. Lower interest rates stimulate the economy because they cause the value of the dollar to decline. Lower interest rates cause consumers to spend more. They encourage business to incur debt to expand their businesses. Because the dollar is less valuable it makes American produced products less expensive in the world marketplace. American stocks gain in value. Exporters' stocks gain in value and importers' stock suffer.

China resists allowing their money, the yuan, to float freely. This causes the yuan to be undervalued making Chinese imports to other countries cheaper than they naturally should be. As yuan is allowed to be more valuable the Chinese economy will most likely suffer. China has begun a policy of encouraging consumption of their domestic products, hoping to gradually decrease the economic impact of losing exports. If China and Japan begin reducing their holdings of U.S. debt, this will make their currency more valuable and the dollar less valuable. As this happens, the American worker will become more competitive in the World economy. It also may reduce the purchasing power of the American consumer.

The second avenue to fairer trade relationships is to construct trade agreements that push for higher wages in our trading partners' economies and emphasis put on the importance of purchasing more American produced products. There is a natural inclination to be more nationalistic in our thinking and be against free trade. If we follow this path, the consequences would be fewer exports sold overseas.

The issues are complex. The answers are not clear. This is why investors must not read the news to prove their views are correct and others are not so correct. Few read the news with the attitude: How does the news affect my investments? Most people cling to economic views much like I cling to supporting Nebraska Cornhuskers' football team. I am Cornhusker for no other reason than I grew up in Nebraska cheering for them. (I do admit I have lost many of my ingrained Cornhusker values over the years). Clinging to long-held opinions when reading the news will cause one to miss information that can help one to be a better investor. News is important. It also must be read trying to understand the direction of the economy. Failing to do this, golden opportunities will be missed.

We must learn to be humble and always consider the fact we may be wrong. Look beyond what we think we know. We always must be asking, "Am I paying attention to factual financial information or am I letting political, community, business and religious biases blind me?" Be on the lookout for information that indicates a stock's earnings are threatened. It's the best way to avoid a mistake.

PUTTING IT ALL TOGETHER

I HEAR THE stories. Some person who knows little about stocks just happens to buy the right stock and becomes an instant millionaire. I want emphasize I hear the stories. I have never really met a person who did that. I have known people who for a lifetime have been extremely successful in their business or professional careers. They decided to invest in the stock market. Then in a very short period of time, they lost a lot of their savings. It is amazing to spend a lifetime being very careful, learning a business, making good decisions and then seemingly blow it recklessly without much thought or understanding what drives their decision making. Many setting out to make investments in the stock market forget they are beginners in a new endeavor. One has to understand what they are doing and why they are doing it if they want to avoid a disaster. Here are some rules I have put together that are necessary to follow if one is to hope to be successful in the stock market:

Be willing to invest in the right equipment. It is important to buy a computer and be connected to the Internet. Stock-picking software is essential. The software should have the broadest options possible to set the criteria for sorting out all the stocks available. The software should have back testing capabilities. Back testing should be done constantly trying out new and old theories. This will give you a good understanding of the ebbs and flows of the market. Without a good understanding of the market, one will never overcome letting emotions creep into your decision making.

Learn to recognize the stock and market characteristics that will lead to the best returns. I have learned earnings, growth of earnings per share and safety are the best protection I have against sudden adversity. You need to convince yourself what the important stock characteristics are that work the best for you. You need to be comfortable with your choices otherwise you will find sudden adversity will defeat you. I also look for stocks with consistent price growth. When a stock has a choppy up-and-down price patterns, it is easy to be caught zigging when you should be zagging. You need to have a feel for the rhythms of the stock market, so you can be patient and you can be bolder at other times. Pay particular attention to the presidential term charts. The stocks with the correct stock characteristics give the best chance for success, but you also need to pay attention to the stock market cycle. It is difficult to make a profit if you are buying stocks when the market is peaking. You will be spinning your wheels if you find yourself selling when the market is bottoming out.

Set reasonable goals with longer time frames. If your picks are successful seven or eight times out of ten that is being extremely successful. In fact, I have had very profitable years where only 50% of my stocks showed a gain. Many stock prices will double and more in a year's time. A thirty percent overall growth is exceptional. Set rules that you have back-tested when you should buy and when you should sell. Stick to the rules. **Be picky. Be sticky.** Don't panic over a bad day, week or even a month. Think in longer time frames. The market over the years has trended up. Down years are seldom and they are always followed by a vigorous up year. I have prepared charts on the following pages to show my grandsons the importance of setting money aside every month and how compound interest will reward you with sizeable returns in a forty year period.

Pay attention to what you know will work. Back testing is the proof of what works and what doesn't. Listening to experts and not back testing is a formula for failure. A lot is lost when listening to the experts. One has to be sure that you understand them completely. What works for a short period of time often does not work over the long haul. You must stick with strategies that work year in and year out.

Be diversified. Never invest more than 10% in any one stock or industry. Better yet, limit it to 5%. Putting your eggs in one basket can lead to either spectacular or disastrous results. Over time you will experience both. Spectacular is rewarding. A small one stock disaster could wipe you out completely if your eggs are in one basket.

Be wary of buying on the margin. Borrowing money in an up market will lead to more profits. Borrowing money in a down market can wipe you out and then some. Margin calls that force decision making is bad. Buying on the margin even in a slightly down market can cause emotions to take over. In an up market buying on the margin can cause over confidence.

Go with proven earnings performance. Talking about the latest new product makes the conversation about the future exciting. Until profits start rolling, there is no way from an investment viewpoint to know if the product will be a success. The idea is to avoid making mistakes that will reduce your profits. The difference between a good golfer and a bad golfer is not how far a golfer can hit a ball. The difference is consistently making par or better or the total number of stokes taken. Good management and making consistent profits is a better story than the products produced. Basing decisions on earnings yields and growth of earnings over many years are the better bet, rather than gambling whether a new product will be a success.

Don't let your politics blind your judgment. Most all stock market failures have been the result of private sector failures. The crashes of 1929 and 2008 were the result of the over extension of private debt—railroad bonds in 1929, home mortgages in 2008. Deregulation was the cause of the Savings and Loan crisis in the 1980's. In my insurance industry under pricing policies and poor investment decisions have been the cause time after time of serious insurance company financial problems causing mass cancellations and bankruptcies. Even as I write this, there are increasing articles about companies extending more and less creditworthy loans to prop up declining sales. In the past, many recessions were caused by bloated inventories. Always watch for building systemic problems in the private sector.

Be able to back up what you are doing or thinking with words. If you decide to buy or sell a stock, spell out the reasons in writing. This is an important method to hold yourself responsible. Keep a written diary of your activities. Go back and review the diary. You can see when you were right and when you made a decision based on poor information. Success comes from experience.

Stick with it from beginning to end. The following two pages are charts I made for my two grandsons, Quintin and Colton. The charts show two options: first investing $24,000 at age 23; the second putting away $50 a month for five years, then raising it to $200 a month. If you stick with it doing either, it will lead to millions at a fairly young age. If this is not evidence enough, consider the story of Jack Rupert MacDonald, a life-long government Seattle attorney, who amassed a fortune of $184,000,000 sticking to his investment program. This is not an amount you would expect from someone living off a government salary all his life. When he died he left his fortune to the Seattle community.

There is more to life than working 8 to 5. Community service, reading and traveling are far more exciting ways to spend your life than trying to climb the corporate ladder. Of course many over the years have accused me of being a small town guy. I guess I am, but that doesn't mean you have to be satisfied with a small World.

Finally, for people my age, retiring means something different today than in years past. It is a chance for a second career. Even though I have turned seventy, I believe I can and I want to make a difference. That is possible because my physical and mental health are very good. If I eat my fruit and vegetables, don't take up smoking and drinking and exercise regularly, I have a good chance of seeing ninety. Our investment goals should reflect a longer life span. We should be investing in stocks that have an excellent chance of growing.

My hope this book will get you thinking and get you on the path of paying attention to the statistics that count.

Invest $20,000 at age twenty-two at 22% per year average growth.

Age	Balance
23	$ 24,000
24	29,768
25	36,316
26	44,306
27	54,054
28	65,946
29	80,454
30	98,154
31	119,748
32	146,092
33	178,233
34	217,444
35	265,282
36	323,644
37	394,845
38	481,711
39	587,688
40	716,979
41	874,715
42	1,067,152
43	1,301,926
44	1,588,350
45	1,917,787
46	2,364,100
47	2,884,202
48	3,518,727

DONALD L. HINMAN

1. Invest $50 a month for five years into a savings account paying 1% interest.
2. After five years raise the monthly amount to $100 a month at 23% average growth.
3. After ten years raise the monthly amount to $200 a month.

Age	Balance
23	$ 603
24	1,202
25	1,827
26	2,449
27	3,077
28	5,092
29	7,551
30	10,555
31	14,211
32	18,676
33	25,462
34	43,841
35	56,163
36	71,197
37	89,537
38	111,913
39	139,211
40	179,515
41	213,146
42	262,715
43	323,190
44	396,969
45	486,980

ABOUT DON HINMAN

D ON AND HIS wife Helen have lived in Yakima, Washington for over forty years. Helen is a retired school counselor. In the mid-1980's she was honored by the National Association of School Counselors for her work with students who had learning disabilities.

Don and Helen have two sons, Ron and Tom, and two grandsons, Quintin and Colton. They have raised twenty-one foster children and opened their home to nine foreign exchange students. They have visited in each of the exchange students' homes in their own countries.

Don attended Hastings College in Nebraska and graduate school at the University of Nebraska. His major fields of studies were economics, accounting and law.

Don is an insurance broker and the president of Mid-Valley Insurance, Inc. For twenty years he was the managing partner of H&H Property Management specializing in owning and renting residential houses, apartment complexes and office buildings.

Don was a co-founder of Yakima Neighborhood Health Services and for the last thirty-five years, been its board chairman. Yakima Neighborhood Health Services is a large medical, dental and mental health clinic with multiple locations in the Yakima Valley. In 2015 at its national convention in Orlando, the National Association of Community Health Centers awarded Don the Aaron L. Brown Memorial Public Service Award.

Don has served on the Yakima City Council.

Printed in the United States
By Bookmasters